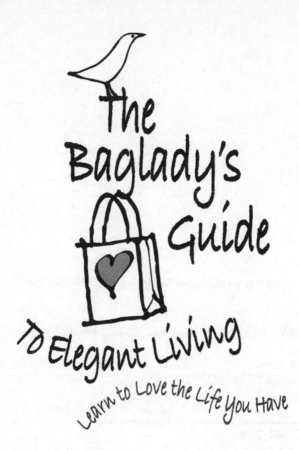

# The Baglady's Guide To Elegant Living

## Learn to Love the Life You Have

### Dina Dove

**Health Communications, Inc.**
Deerfield Beach, Florida

*www.hcibooks.com*

**Library of Congress Cataloging-in-Publication Data**

Dove, Dina.
    The baglady's guide to elegant living : learn to love the life you have / Dina
Dove.
      p.  cm.
    ISBN-10: 0-7573-0722-1 (trade paper)
    ISBN-13: 978-0-7573-0722-5 (trade paper)
    1. Self-help technïques. 2. Self-esteem. 3. Women—Psychology. I. Title.

BF632.D68  2008
158.1—dc22

                                             2008008852

Publisher: Health Communications, Inc.
            3201 S.W. 15th Street
            Deerfield Beach, FL 33442-8190

*Cover image by Rod Dutton*
*Cover design by Larissa Hise Henoch*
*Interior design and formatting by Lawna Patterson Oldfield*

*Dedicated to the*
*memory of my grandmother,*
*Rose Neil Dove*
*1893–1973*

# Introduction

It was an unseasonably cold spring morning, just this side of winter. The drizzling, wet mist added to the chill. Of course, I had left my umbrella at home. Drenched and shivering there on the bench, I looked like a wet dog with hair matted to my forehead. Completely deflated, I had no energy to move—the weather mirrored my state of mind.

My life as I knew it was over; systematically, one after another, all the things on which I based my self-worth were gone.

My work.

My money.

My honor.

My marriage.

My car was the only thing I had left to my name . . . and it was acting like it would be the next to go.

Even the possibility for the future was gone, because I wasn't just starting over with nothing. Thanks to high overhead and an unexpected downturn in the economy, I was forced to sell the business to which I had devoted my life at a huge loss. I was a quarter million dollars in debt, and for the second time in six weeks, the IRS had robbed my checking account of its last $50.

I had nothing to do, no one to turn to; so there I sat, completely lost in despair.

# Chapter 1

I don't know exactly when she showed up, but something seemed to suddenly take the chill off, and I was nudged out of my funk for a moment. I looked to my left, and there she sat, perfectly still, gazing sweetly into space.

I couldn't help but wonder about this little, old lady. She must have been at least eighty years old. The weather was lousy, but she looked picture perfect.

A slight lady with lips pursed in a modest smile, she wasn't wet or cold. Her huge umbrella could have sheltered at least three people. She held herself erect, certainly a woman of dignity and grace. She looked like a classic grandma from the 1950s. Covering her snowy white hair was a dainty felt hat with a mesh net across her forehead. Her light blue spring coat covered a brightly flowered voile dress. She wore thick-heeled pumps. Indicative of the days of garter belts and non-stretch hose, her nylons showed subtle little ripples at her ankles. She smelled of lavender.

The large shopping bag at her feet was just begging to be snatched by the first thief to run through the park. I immediately felt protective of her. Clearly, she had no idea how to take care of herself. Considering the way I looked, she should have worried about *me* taking her bag, but she seemed totally oblivious to any threat to her safety.

"I'd keep that bag a little closer, if I were you," I said flatly.

She leaned over and patted my hand. Her own fragile and wrinkled hands were as soft as silk. "Don't worry, dear. It will be all right."

We sat on the bench, not another word between us until she got up some time later to leave. She smiled sweetly and proclaimed, "This was such a lark. I do hope to see you again sometime." And with that, she was off, clomping softly away, her shopping bag in tow.

The chill seemed to return suddenly, so I bent over to

retie my shoes before running back to the loft. Even that wasn't mine anymore. Due to the lapse in mortgage payments, foreclosure was eminent. The drawn-out legal process may buy me another month or two at best.

# Chapter 2

S ince I was broke, with nothing better to do, I spent a lot of time running. Running and thinking. Actually, wallowing in self-pity was more like it. I thought it would help me get back in shape while taking my mind off my problems. In years gone by when I ran, I could get in the zone and feel so free. So I drove myself to find that place of abandon again, but to no avail. Now running had become its own hell. No matter how I fought to avoid it, all I did was relive the past over and over again in my head, reminding myself of all the ways I'd fallen short.

Today was no different. *You stupid, stupid idiot,* I berated myself once again. *How has my life been reduced to this mess?* Trudging on, I worked hard to empty my mind. For a few minutes, I was successful.

I slowed down to a walk. It was then that I noticed the bright splash of color through the trees. That little, old lady was in the park again. Her back was to me, but I would recognize that umbrella anywhere.

Seeing the "baglady" took my mind off my troubles for a few minutes. *It's truly ludicrous, this label I've given her, and all because of that shopping bag. I wonder why she's there on that bench again. It doesn't add up, her hanging around in the park like this. She looks like the type of woman who would be on the arm of a princely older gentleman, a man who would open doors for her and even throw his cape over a puddle, so her feet would not be muddied. She certainly seems like she's been cherished in her day. I wonder where her prince is now.*

With that, my mind wandered back to the man, my exhusband, who had once cherished me. We had been high-school sweethearts. Well, not at first. Actually, at first he hated me. I was a headstrong, no-nonsense young woman. I worked at night and slept through history class where

Craig sat behind me. One day he banged my chair with his foot, and I woke up with a start, turned around, and told him off. That was his story. I didn't even remember it.

The following summer, when I was sixteen, I changed jobs to work at McDonald's, and we ended up working together, much to his chagrin. Since he was the best at counter sales, Craig was chosen to train me. He had won all the sales contests until I came on the scene.

Soon after that, he was promoted to the lead position. I appreciated the fact that even after I stole some of his glory, he still treated me fairly, and I found myself attracted to him. We flirted a little bit, and eventually I asked him to the Sadie Hawkins dance. After that we were an item.

He liked me, but his parents didn't approve. I was from the wrong side of the tracks. I wasn't good enough for their son. But no matter what they did to break us up, our bond grew stronger. I followed him to college, and we were married during our second year.

In our early twenties, we started our first business, moving across the country three times in pursuit of entrepreneurial and financial success. He had never wanted children, so our business and our employees became our children. Craig just loved being a business owner. And I loved Craig.

But over the years, we grew apart. And, in the end, the only thing we had in common was the business. When the business was sold, there was nothing left of the couple who had once been so in love. After twenty years of marriage, it was over.

So many regrets. *We should have had children. We should have paid more attention to our personal lives, to each other, but our careers, our success, took all our effort.*

I always thought we could weather any storm. I saw other marriages split up after the kids left home, and I swore that would never happen to us. I thought not having children would save us, but it snuck up on us like a thief in the night.

The pulling apart was so gradual. As it turned out, work had the same effect on us as children had on some of our friends. When all our energy was put on other things, and little attention was focused on the relationship, it disintegrated, so slowly, so silently. I didn't realize it was dying until it was already dead.

Oh, there were warnings, but I refused to see them. Betsy and I had been friends forever. On one of her visits she told me that she thought Craig was having an affair. But at the time, I was so sure of him that I just thought she had been reading too many romance novels.

Later, one of my employees told me that the production crew thought that Craig and I had a "marriage of convenience." Still, I thought it was everyone else who was blind instead of me. What a fool I was.

Even now, I have a memory of the love and longing that was once there, but it's only a memory. We didn't want the same things anymore. In fact, our wants and needs became so different that it was impossible to stay together. It's sad. I know our time together is over, but I still remember the boy with whom I fell in love all those years ago. That boy is gone, and, sadly, that girl is gone, too.

I don't know how long I had been walking and reliving this failure in my life when I noticed that the day had all but passed. My heart had broken as the marriage began to unravel, but the final filings and signing of the divorce decree had devastated me. Hope for love everlasting was soon replaced with bitterness and loneliness. So much for running to get my mind off things! I practically dragged myself back home in a depressed stupor.

By the time I got back to the loft, I was starving. Pulling a cheap TV dinner out of the freezer, I slid it in the microwave, opened a can of Coke, and just sat there. The timer went off. Mechanically, I pulled out my supper, peeled back

the top, took one look at the institutional square tray and
the empty chair across from me, and turned my eyes to the
ceiling. *Why me?*

# Chapter 3

After a restless night, I was back in the park again, running hard, trying not to think. All yesterday had done was bring me down. *I have to stop thinking and get in the zone. Come on, zone! Come on, before I have to start thinking again.*

*I ought to call my parents and tell them the divorce is final . . . and that I've lost my job, but I just can't deal with Dad's attitude that nothing I do is ever good enough. I also can't bear to hear the disappointment in Mom's voice.*

*Mom and Dad are probably eating breakfast right now, wondering why I haven't called them back. The other day, I* called and left them a message when I knew they would be out. It was very lighthearted, as lighthearted as I could be, telling them that I was taking a little break from work and not to worry, I'd be in touch soon. I rationalized that I needed to work through it on my own before dragging my parents into the mess.

Thinking about my parents and my internal struggle of whether to call them started a whole new flood of emotions. Memories of my childhood came to add fuel to an already raging fire. Yes, we had been extremely poor with seven people packed into a little two-bedroom duplex. It was Mom who coined the phrase "the poverty area" because she didn't like thinking we lived in the "slums." Racial riots and knife fights on the bus were nothing out of the ordinary. The parents from other neighborhoods didn't want their kids associating with us. Today, the newer residents call it the "'hood." Gangs now rule those streets.

I was so ashamed of our family situation. I begged my mom and dad to move. I worked my whole life to get out of there, to get past my past. *I can't go back. I won't go back to that place.*

*I just can't handle talking to them now, hearing them tell me to come home. There's no way I'm going back there, no matter what.* With each step I took, my rage was building. *Why did this have to happen to me?*

Just then, a raised section of the sidewalk caught my foot, and in a moment I was on the ground. Stunned, I sat there assessing the damage. My right elbow was only scraped a little, but my left knee was bleeding. I got up and limped to the closest bench. The flow of blood from my knee was just about to hit the top of my sock. *I need a Kleenex, quick.*

I felt a slight tap on my arm, and a hand held out a little pack of those travel tissues. I was so involved with the blood and pain that I didn't even look up. I just grabbed the gift given to me and started to nurse my wounds.

The sting and the throbbing took all my attention. As I got the blood under control, I took several slow, deep breaths that helped me calm down a bit, and I felt my heartbeat slowing. I pulled off my shoe and sock to take a look at my ankle, hoping it wasn't too swollen. Fortunately, after massaging it for a few minutes, and standing up on it again, there was no pain.

It was only then that I took a look at the now empty tissue pack. I looked around quickly, but no one was there. Walking out to the main sidewalk that ran along the street,

I looked up and down the lane. There wasn't anyone who looked like they might have been the tissue fairy. *Hmm. That's weird*, I thought.

With that, I tossed the empty package in the trash and walked toward home. My wounds needed cleaning and some antiseptic cream.

# Chapter 4

I t was sunny the next day as I jogged past the bench I'd tripped in front of on Monday. *There she is again,* I thought. *The first day I saw the baglady that umbrella seemed huge, but I'm taken aback by the actual size of it now. Today, it is just a little parasol. Same markings, but I could swear it is only about half the size. Man, can I be losing my mind on top of everything else I've lost? And there is that bag again. She is definitely asking for trouble with the way she doesn't keep it close. I better keep an eye on her. She's totally defenseless out here.*

In one movement, I dropped to the bench and scooted that bag up against her, tucking the handles in close before she had time to protest.

"Hello, my dear. I see you are recovering nicely from your fall," she commented. I looked at her, surprised. "Was that you who handed me the tissues yesterday after I fell? When I looked up, no one was there. How did you do that?"

Ignoring me, she continued, "Isn't it simply a delightful spring day?"

After hesitating, I had to give in. "Yeah, I guess so." Her cheerfulness made it almost impossible to maintain my foul mood.

"I'm so glad you are here. I brought a story for you." With that, she dug deep into the bag and pulled out a disheveled mess of pages, some cut from magazines, others on typing paper. Mixed in were several index cards with what looked like little sayings on them.

She pondered over this page and that, seeming to skim them to find just the right one. Finally, she separated out a page, straightening out the wrinkles as if to make it more presentable for me. Then she folded it slowly and deliberately into a little square that fit in the palm of her hand. Pleased with her work and no longer preoccupied, she turned all her attention back to me.

"But never mind this for the moment," she said. "I hope I am not intruding, and please tell me if I am . . . but, dear, do tell me how a beautiful young lady with her whole life ahead of her can be so unhappy?"

At forty, I didn't feel young, but I suppose at her age I was just that. And . . . what about my demeanor gave away my misery? I wasn't sure if I wanted anyone to know my terrible situation. Being a failure was so humiliating. After a long silence, I decided to tell her my dismal story. I hate whiners, and now I had become one, but this lady seemed like she really wanted to know.

"My whole life I have done what I was supposed to," I explained. "I have always worked hard. In fact, I've been working ever since I was fourteen. I started my first business when I was twenty-four, followed all the rules, and now I have nothing.

"Until now, I have always been able to figure out how to win. No matter what the obstacle, I could overcome it to meet my goal. I started my company thirteen years ago and built it day by day, year after year, reinvesting until it finally paid off. Over the years, I became a successful designer and manufacturer. I was at the top of my game. I went from childhood poverty to successful entrepreneur, but now I'm in worse shape than when I started."

"It sounds like you had some great accomplishments. Let me ask you, were you happy?"

I almost rolled my eyes. *That question is totally irrelevant. Here I am drowning in debt and despair, and she is asking if I was happy when I was rich and powerful. What does happiness have to do with it? I was* successful. *I was respected in my field and making great profits. And wasn't that what I had worked so hard for?*

I didn't want to snap at her. My predicament was certainly not her fault, and she had listened to me complain for quite a while. She didn't deserve the wrath I was feeling. So I concentrated on calming myself down while looking for a tactful way to answer her. The silence extended for so long that she was the first to speak again.

Haltingly and with great compassion, she asked, "What I mean is, were you really and truly happy . . . on the inside?"

Those last three words, "on the inside," made me think. I had really made it to the big time. But I had never figured out how to have a life at the same time. My work was my life, and I was so determined to be successful that I had on blinders of solid steel. My focus was 100 percent.

Then I paused and allowed it to sink in deep. The truth is . . . I had hated my business. Every evening for years, after everyone was gone and the factory was empty, I would go into my ritual tirade with God. Even though I hated the business, I felt like *he* was holding me there for some reason. My secret life, totally aside from the persona of the happy and successful businessperson, played itself out at night in a lonely factory in a fight against the universe. Pleading, crying, and finally yelling at God for answers, "Why, why, *why* do I have to do this?"

And he never answered. I would make deals with him and later demands on him about how much longer I would stay. He didn't cooperate with any of my plans. I was tortured by the feeling that there was a purpose. And yet, not having any idea what that purpose was, it all seemed so meaningless.

And now, looking back, I particularly regretted my life. Even in my success, I had been terribly unhappy. If only I had realized how hollow it would be, I never would have spent my life that way.

I was so burned out and couldn't imagine starting all over again. Besides, what would be the use? Everyone wanted a piece of me. No matter what I did, there was no way out.

Falling deep into my own thoughts, I don't know how long I sat there. By the time I resurfaced, the sun was low in the sky. The baglady was still sitting there on the bench, her hands folded neatly in her lap. How long had she been sitting silently there beside me? It was as if she was a witness to the pain in my heart, but I hadn't spoken a word.

Her kindness overwhelmed me, and I started sobbing. She pulled a perfectly folded linen handkerchief out of that big bag of hers, handed it to me, and put her arm around my shoulder. Even though dark would soon overtake us, she seemed to have no care for the time and did not rush me. When I finally pulled myself together and felt ready to go, I asked if I could walk her home, but she said she would be meeting a friend close by for dinner. She gently tucked the paper she had folded up a lifetime ago into my hand and sent me on my way.

At home over a cup of spice tea, I unfolded the paper the baglady had given me. It had been torn out haphazardly from a magazine more than twenty years ago. *Had it been in that bag ever since then? Possibly. It sure looks well read.*

Right before you were born, God placed in your right hand a brand-new artist's canvas, rolled up like a scroll. And in your left, a handful of brightly colored paints. He hugged you tightly and kissed you on the forehead. "Go into the world, my child, and make of your life a beautiful masterpiece."

Shocked at the sight of a newborn armed with such sophisticated materials, the doctor pried your little fingers from the gifts you were born with to your screams of protest.

"A baby cannot possibly have the skills to paint on canvas with oils."

Soon these gifts were replaced with a page outlined with soft blue lines, each with a number in it, and crayons labeled with matching numbers. As they tucked these in your crib, you were assured, "Life is about staying in the lines and painting by the numbers. If you do that, everything will work out fine."

And that is a lie!

—Author Unknown

*What can she possibly be saying? That everything I was ever taught and lived by is a lie? In my opinion, she is being a hypocrite. Clearly, the baglady is the picture of the establishment: prim, proper, perfectly poised. If anyone colors in the lines, she does!*

# Chapter 5

I was still irritated the next time I saw her. "What are you trying to tell me?" I demanded, ready to pounce on her the moment she answered.

"Life doesn't really work the way you think it does." Her tone was gentle yet completely self-assured.

I was fully prepared to defend my way of thinking. After all, if what I lived my whole life for had been a lie, what could I hold on to? I was already at the end of my rope.

"It's certainly worked for you!" I blurted out, immediately ashamed of the attitude I rolled into that statement.

She smiled as if I had paid her a compliment. There was a lilt in her voice as she started to speak. She clearly found my insolence amusing. "You remind me so much of myself at your age. It's like looking in a mirror. I was so angry. I thought the whole world was against me. Those were dark days." She dropped into silence, seeming to relive it.

The whole thing confused me. Then, just as suddenly as she had dived into the pool of past despair, she came out of it, looked at me with determination and clarity of purpose, and said, "I think that might have been the biggest blessing of my entire life!"

Clearly, the woman was crazy, but then I have always liked people who are a little out of the ordinary. So I egged her on a little more. "How? Why? What do you mean?" I fumbled.

"You see, I was absolutely forced to give up on the things that I thought would bring me happiness. All my life, I had done exactly what my upbringing had taught me . . . and like you, it all came crashing down."

Then, with renewed spunk, she flashed a huge ear-to-ear grin. Slapping her hand to her knee for emphasis and full of delight, she declared again with enthusiasm, "Yep! Best thing that ever happened to me!"

Inside this little lady's delicate frame lived a ball of fire.

What a strange case she was.

*Never mind her. I have plans of my own. I already have my few remaining possessions packed in my car. I am leaving this city behind me. Packing it in. Moving out. Running from the hell that is my life, from the memories, the broken promises, the life gone cold.*

"Look," I blurted out, "I'm out of here. I've got my stuff packed. I'm heading out, and I may never come back!"

I paused a moment, but she made no move to argue with me. "I'm glad you have your sweet, little life where everything turns out perfect. Good for you!"

*What on earth has gotten into me? Now I have to be mean to a frail, old lady. What a great person I've turned out to be,* I berated myself.

The baglady? She remained completely warm and yet strangely detached all at the same time.

Turning around to face me, she took both of my hands in hers. Her clear blue eyes were filled with compassion. Practically everyone I had known had turned on me when things went south. And yet in my darkest moment, she was there, giving me permission to rail at the world and to run if that is what I truly wanted. She looked at me with such acceptance. The feeling was mesmerizing.

"My dear? My dear . . . you know," she started slowly, trying to get my attention, "you may leave if you want to. But
do keep in mind that you will be taking yourself with you
wherever you go." Her words shook me back into reality
and back to the awareness that I had just told her I was running away, driving off into the sunset, never to look back.

She squeezed my hands, presented an index card from her
bag, smiled gently, and then settled back on the bench again.

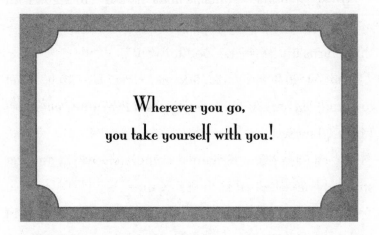

**W**herever you go,
you take yourself with you!

Panic overcame me. I didn't know what to do. I thought
I had it all figured out. Get out of Dodge. Leave the past
and everything attached to it behind.

I had to get away quickly. I felt totally unnerved. My
mind screamed, *Run!* And in a moment I was out of there,

running deep into the park, not daring to look back.

I was breathless by the time I circled around and got back to the loft. Determined not to let anything change my mind about leaving, I quickly checked to make sure everything was turned off and unplugged, made a quick trip to the bathroom, and ran down to the parking garage.

Unlocking the car, I realized that I still had the card that bizarre lady had given me. Just to get it out of my hand, I attached it to the visor. "Wherever you go, you take yourself with you."

*Yeah, right. And right now I'm going to take myself to Phoenix to see Ellen. We were pretty close in college, and she's going through a bad divorce, too. We can tar and feather the masculine gender together. Maybe that will make me feel better. At least I'll have someone to commiserate with.*

I buckled up, turned the key, and prepared for my escape. The car didn't start. The engine barely turned over once. With the next twist of the key, there was nothing but a clicking sound. I swore through clenched teeth. "Great, now my battery is dead!"

# Chapter 6

**P**ar for the course, the battery wasn't the only problem. Determined to drive to Phoenix, I hung out in the garage waiting for another resident to arrive on the scene. If we could push my car out to meet up close enough, I could pull the jumper cables out of the trunk and still get out of town by the end of the day.

Everything went according to plan. Within an hour, I was revving up the engine and ready to take off again. Fresh from its latest influx of juice, everything seemed to be in order. I was feeling victorious as I pulled away from the city just before the afternoon traffic started to swell. I switched on the radio and even sang along. When I had finished the second song, the radio suddenly went dead.

*Oh, well,* I thought. *I can do without the music.*

A few minutes later, I heard a couple of unusual sounds, kind of like the slipping of gears. With that, I rubbed the dashboard and talked real sweet to the car. "Come on, baby. Just make it to Phoenix. That's all I ask."

Ten minutes later and twenty miles out of town, the car made another set of clicking noises, the fan on the air conditioner stopped, and the engine went dead. I was able to coast off the highway before the tires rolled to a stop. Then I coaxed and pleaded with the car to start again, but it was only those faithful clicks I heard each time I tried the ignition.

Just five minutes later, a guy stopped to help. "Sounds like your alternator to me, ma'am. You're gonna need to get it towed back to town. I'll give them a call for you."

I was defeated. So much for getting out of town. I couldn't afford the tow truck, much less the price of an alternator. "Don't bother. I don't have any cash for the tow, and I certainly don't have the money to fix whatever's broken," I said gruffly.

But before I could stop him, he told me the truck was

already on the way. I didn't know how I was going to pay, but the driver told me he would let me leave it on his lot for a few days and agreed to take direct payment from my insurance for the towing charge. When we got to the lot, he cautioned me, "You ought to take all your personal things out of the car since it might be here awhile."

The thought of toting all my stuff back up the three flights of stairs to the loft just added to the frustration of my day. After emptying the back seat and trunk, I went through the console and glove box and pulled everything off the visors. There was that stupid card again.

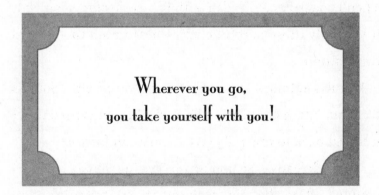

Wherever you go,
you take yourself with you!

*Well, I sure won't have to worry about taking myself with me anywhere now, will I?*

# Chapter 7

S tuck in town, the only escape I had was to try again to find some solace in running. So it was back to the park the very next day, but I was determined to stay away from that old lady.

I stayed clear of her for a week, running far enough back in the park so that she would not see me, but close enough that I could catch a glimpse of the park bench from the path. Every day she was on that bench, talking with passersby or reading or rummaging through her bag. Even though I always looked for her, it was strangely unsettling to see her there.

The baglady was still a sitting duck for anyone wanting to snatch her things, but she remained oblivious to the dangers.

One day, I spotted her on my way into the park, but on my way out, I noticed that she was gone. She must have left early, so I circled back around to the route that would bring me right past her bench.

There was something on the bench, flapping in the breeze, so I ran over to take a closer look. Maybe she had left a scarf or her hanky. There, stuck to the bench with a bright pink pushpin, was a sheet of lacy stationery. Handwritten in a dainty but shaky cursive, it could only be the writing of the baglady. I shook my head in wonder. *She is full of surprises, this one.*

Leaning over, I could see that it was another one of her "stories." Pulling the pin out of the wood and grabbing the page, I could not resist sitting down to read it.

There was a sentinel standing at the gates of the city. A man, a newcomer to the town, all his possessions stacked high upon his cart, a donkey at the harness, stopped to have a word with him.

He greeted the sentinel with a broad smile, inquiring about the town he was about to enter. "Please, sir, do tell me about your town, its people, and the life I could expect here."

"Please tell me, if you will, what was your previous village like?" inquired the sentinel. At that, the traveler spoke at length about the prosperous and happy life he had in his last home.

The sentinel, a man of few words, waved him into the city gates. "You will find our town much like the one you lived in before. Welcome, new neighbor."

About an hour later, another man came to the gates. His ass seemed to be out of sorts as he was cracking the whip and cursing at the animal. While inquiring about the town he was about to enter, the sentinel once again asked what his experiences were in his last home.

Noticeably irritated, he complained, "It was an awful place to live. Bad economy and unfriendly people. That is why I am here, so I might find something better."

"I'm sorry to tell you this, but you will find our village to be much like the one you left."

# Chapter 8

**H**ow does she know I'm still here? That's what I want to know.

I was immediately angry, but I took the new story home with me and made an effort to calm down. Later on that evening, I read it again, pondering the connection between it and the earlier index card. This time, her message came through loud and clear, and it infuriated me. *She is telling me that I have a bad attitude. But after what I have been through, I think I have a right to be unhappy.*

The next morning, I jumped in the shower, grabbed a cup of coffee, and set off with determination to find that baglady and have a few words with her. And yet, as I got closer to the park, I was almost embarrassed.

She was looking away from me as I approached, so I slowed my pace until I stopped. I didn't want to startle her, and I was not completely sure that I'd be welcome. If she had abandoned me like I did her, it would have been over. So I paused to see what her reaction would be when she looked my way.

When she turned and saw me, her whole face lit up. She enthusiastically patted the seat next to her, and I didn't hesitate to take it.

The baglady let me talk on and on. When I paused, she waited patiently to allow me to continue if there was something else I needed to say. She let me vent my anger and frustration with the things she had said and written. Even though it was now clear that she had known all along, I confessed that I had been watching her in the park and struggling to understand the things we had talked about. She just smiled, sincerely pleased to have me back.

"You seem to know exactly what I need . . . and . . . I don't even know your name."

She almost giggled. "Well," she started, totally amused, "now that you ask, my name is Rose."

So used to introducing myself in a professional manner, I extended my right hand as I spoke, "I'm Angela." Then after hesitating, I continued, "Rose, you seem like you care about me specifically. I don't get that."

She set her gaze across the street somewhere. Clearly, she had no intention of helping me out on this. She was with me. She wasn't ignoring me; she just wasn't answering.

After a long silence, she finally spoke, changing the subject. "Dear, tell me, aside from your troubles lately, what have you been thinking about? Do you recall?"

"Well, for the past week, since I told you I was leaving, and you told me . . . well . . . I taped the card you gave me on the mirror, and I have been thinking about what you said. It was such a strange thing to say. You seemed so cryptic that . . . well . . . I've been trying to figure out what you really meant by that. And . . . you don't know this, but the day I met you was the first time I'd ever run through this part of the park. Then I saw you here. It is all so strange. I never pay attention to anybody when I am out. They are all like a big blur in the background of my thoughts about all the things I normally am worrying over. But you stuck out like a sore thumb. You looked like a mugging waiting to happen."

She smiled, not looking directly at me, but certainly listening intently to what I was saying. "You are very perceptive, aren't you?" she asked thoughtfully.

"Well, I wouldn't really say that," I answered. "It took me quite a while to figure out what you told me. But I spent a lot of time thinking about it. In fact, I didn't even get it until you left that story for me on the bench yesterday. What you said to me, and what the story was conveying, were obviously the same thing. So I went home and really thought about it.

"I have to admit that I have been so busy wondering about this unusual chain of events that I haven't been thinking about my other problems as much. Instead of being angry all the time, I have been busy trying to understand what you were telling me."

"Ah, yes," she said, "what you focus on expands."

"Anyway, you were telling me, ever so gently that I had a bad attitude and that until I changed my attitude, I would continue to be unhappy no matter where I went. I was really upset with you."

I stopped abruptly, realizing that she had just dropped another odd remark on me. "Hey, what did you mean? What you focus on expands?"

"You just told me that you have been wondering about things," the baglady reminded me. "When you spend time thinking about how unhappy you are, you get to experience more unhappiness.

"When you put your attention on something more positive, what do you get? Something more positive. In this case, you said you have been wondering and . . . trying to understand. Which . . . made you less angry. It was just a small change, but even that made a difference in your life. Don't you see?" She grabbed an index card and slipped it into my hand.

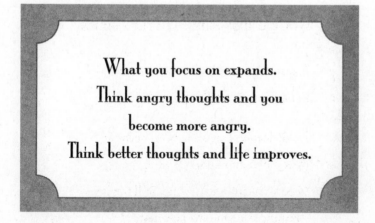

What you focus on expands.
Think angry thoughts and you
become more angry.
Think better thoughts and life improves.

"It's just the way of things," she said. "It's just the way of things."

# Chapter 9

"**D**ear, did it ever cross your mind that your life might have fallen apart for a reason?"

"No."

"Subconsciously, that you might have caused it all to happen?"

"No."

"That maybe it was for the best?"

"*No!*" I was indignant.

She took no offense. But she waited, preoccupied with feeding a bird some breadcrumbs she had pulled out of her bag. Rose seemed to be deep in thought, but I sensed she was feeding the birds to buy a little time before she continued.

She began, "May I tell you something about myself?"

I was taken aback—and actually kind of ashamed of myself. With this dear, old lady, it had always been about me. In my arrogance, I never even considered that she had anything of consequence to share. I was so wrapped up in my own struggles and consumed by what I was going through that I hadn't bothered to think much about her. Rose was old and unassuming. I had clearly prejudged her as "not very interesting." She had just been a listening post for me to take my frustrations out on. My contribution to her was protection. It was a deal I made with myself to justify unloading on her. Ashamed by my former lack of interest in her, she now had my full attention as she started to share a bit of her story.

"Many years ago, my life fell apart much like yours. I, too, was filled with anger and thought that the problem was outside of me. Everyone was against me. I'm way too big of a chicken to ever commit suicide, but I remember thinking that with all my insurmountable problems, it would be so much better for everyone if I were dead.

"At wits' end, with nowhere else to turn, one day I got

down on my knees and prayed like I had never done before. I wanted so much to understand why things were the way they were. The world seemed pretty messed up to me. I began to read the Bible. Surely, the answer was in there somewhere. I spent every spare minute reading and trying desperately to find answers within the pages. I read thousands of verses written on parchment. I knew the words, simple on one level, held a deeper meaning, if only I could find it. So I read painstakingly for months on end. My yearning for the truth drove me on. I think that, more than any other thing, my understanding of the readings somehow taught me to quiet my mind.

"Initially, my mind just wanted to find fault and place blame for the hell that my life had become. Someone had to be responsible, and they should pay. Slowly but surely, the messages I read enticed me to step back from the judgments, anger, and guilt and look at my problems with new eyes to find the meaning behind what I was going through. Once my ego took a backseat, I was free to see some very profound truths.

"Slowly, very, very slowly, I started to see the reasoning behind a world that seemed to throw all kinds of unfairness in my direction. I started to look at how it would have all been different if things had gone the way I would have had them go. I realized there were very important things I learned from those supposedly tragic occurrences.

"This all took me years to see clearly. It seemed like I would touch a little snippet of truth and then fall back into the darkness. But, I'll tell you what. There is nothing like hearing it out of the mouth of a child.

"I met an amazing little girl. Even at five years old, she was wise beyond her years and able to carry on a conversation as if she were an adult. She was carrying a crushing loss on her heart, and as I came to know her better, I realized how lost she felt in a world with no mother. By the time she was seven, we spent a lot of our time together playing a question game. We would take turns coming up with queries to answer. At first, we learned each other's favorite colors and favorite kind of ice cream. Over time, our questions became much more creative, and the answers were quite insightful as to our deeper thoughts on life. Her feelings of loss and wishing she had her mother would work into so many of her answers. I loved her, but no love can replace a mother's love. At least I could listen. When she was with me, we answered those same questions over and over through the years. As she grew up, new answers would emerge. Her answer to 'Who would you most like to have dinner with?' changed from Jesus to her latest favorite pop star; things like that. But longing for the mother she lost was central to many of her answers.

"Then one day came the repeated question that we had answered so many times before. 'If you could change one thing about your past, what would it be?' In the past, her mom would not have died. But now a fourteen-year-old, long-deprived of her mother, she answered, 'You know, I used to wish that mom had never died, and, of course, I would have loved to have had a mother. But now I see that I wouldn't change it, because if everything would have been different, I think that I would not be as strong as I am.'

"Then it hit me. If this motherless child, who had for years suffered the sadness of a loss far more tragic than mine, could see it in a different light, then I had no business holding on to my blame and judgments about a life gone wrong. A child so young had found a way to completely forgive the world her loss. And more remarkably . . . to see a blessing in it.

"She had grown up and learned to take life on its terms. There was forgiveness in her statement and a letting go of what wasn't to be. There was a determination to go forward into the future, to live the life she was given instead of being stuck in the regret of the one that was not hers to have. I, on the other hand, had a lot to learn. Still angry at the circumstances that had stolen the life I believed I had the right to live, I refused to see any good in what I had. I couldn't see what was right in front of me.

"That child shook the self-pity out of me. Some people could get over heartache, and I was determined to be one of them. It was at that point I decided to change, no matter what it took."

The baglady seemed exhausted at having shared so much of herself, but pleased with herself all the same.

She dug through her bag and handed me another index card.

Changing your mind is the most important change you can ever make.

When you change your mind, the whole world changes for you.

"I know what you are thinking," she continued. "You think that that is a bunch of hooey. I remember feeling the exact same way when I first heard it. I always thought of myself as being the flag at the end of the flagpole, being whipped this way and that at the whim of whichever way the wind was blowing. To think I had anything to say about my circumstances sounded preposterous to me. So I don't blame you for thinking I am a little off my rocker. But, just on the outside chance that it is true, would you humor me for a few minutes? Let's see if it could have any validity in your life."

With a sense of mystery and intrigue, she said carefully, "Imagine for a minute that your mind and your thoughts have controlled everything that has happened to you."

"Well, you're right about one thing. I think this is a bunch of hooey, but I'll play along with you. Show me what you've got."

"It will be a lark! You'll see what I mean." She acted as if she had a great surprise waiting for me.

"You told me that you just lost your company, right? Shall we take on that one?"

Suddenly, Rose had turned into a warrior of sorts. It was as if she had mounted her trusty steed and was off to slay a dragon. She started firing out the questions.

"Okay, how many years did you have your company?"

"Thirteen."

"Did you like it? Were you truly happy there?"

It felt like true confession time, so I had to tell her. "No, I hated it. Actually, it is worse than that . . . I was angry with the world, and I hated God for how trapped I felt there. I yelled at him all the time. I kept asking, pleading with him to set me free, year after year. 'Why? Why? Why?' I would plead. He never answered."

"Really? Never? Why didn't you just quit?"

"I didn't want my employees to be hurt. I remember one day I was moaning about my problems when a friend asked me, 'Angela, what do you really want?' That made me think about it, and I realized that I was worried about the employees. I wanted them to be taken care of.

"Anyway, it was really amazing. A couple of weeks after that, totally unsolicited, a man walked into my corporate office and wanted to buy the company. Finally, I thought my prayers had been answered. Everything was going to be okay. But then after he bought it, we couldn't get along, and he fired me."

"Did you want to keep working in the company?"

"No! I wanted out, but in our contract, I had to agree to work for the company for two years. Every day I thought I could not stand it, but I had committed to stay and help in the transition. He was making me crazy."

Rose was beside herself with excitement. I had just told her the devastating story of my life, and she couldn't be more thrilled.

"Goodness gracious! I had no idea that your story was going to be so good. You are going to love this. Watch me repeat it back to you.

"You hated your business. You hated it for years. You always begged God to get you out. You thought he never answered. Maybe the answer was 'Quit!' but you never saw quitting as an option. You wanted someone to come and take care of your employees. So, totally out of the blue, a stranger walks in and wants to buy it. You sell it.

"I have a question for you. Has this man taken care of your employees?"

"Uh-oh, I'm beginning to see a pattern forming. Yes, he has. In fact, he gave them a benefit package better than anything I could ever afford. They all got paid health insurance and 401k plans."

"And then he fired you, right?"

"Right," I said, feeling pleased that things were turning back in my favor.

She could read my mind. "Now, think back. Before he came to buy it, what was your sincere wish? By everything you tell me, you would have quit long ago if it weren't for your employees. You told me that you wanted someone to buy your company and take care of your employees, right?

"Angela . . . you got exactly what you asked for," she said in an excited whisper.

I had to admit she was making sense. It hit me like a ton of bricks, but I continued my protest, "But then he fired me!"

"First off, let me remind you that you did not ask for someone to take care of you. You asked only for the employees to be taken care of. You might keep that in mind next time you orchestrate your outcome so perfectly.

"And second . . . how else was God going to get you out of there? You were under contract!" She raised her hand in the air as if she'd just run fifty yards for a touchdown.

I thought for a long time. I thought about what I had really wanted, back when I was in the company. My company was meaningless to me, making products that were totally unnecessary. I was making gobs of money but had no time to enjoy life. It was an empty existence. And then in that last year, the business had declined dramatically.

Throughout my career, I had put blinders on. No time for family birthday parties, no time to listen to a friend who just needed a loving ear. Heck, no time to even have friends. I was busy being successful, but that wasn't my dream. For years I had been longing not for money and power, but for peace and contentment, for a life with meaning.

"Rose," I began slowly, tears welling up in my eyes, "you know what I really want?"

And just as I was about to tell her, she nodded ever so slightly, as she smiled and dabbed the corners of her eyes with a hanky she pulled out from under her watchband. Somehow, she already knew what my heart yearned for.

It wasn't long before she was rummaging through that bag again. "I have another decoration for your mirror," she giggled like a schoolgirl.

I read the card carefully, and a million questions started running through my head. The biggest one was the question of my lifetime.

"Rose, do you have any idea why I was trapped in that business for so long? I know that life is not about material

> No circumstance needs to change
> for you to be happy.
> However, you might need to change
> your perceptions.
> Choose to see life differently.

goods, and yet I was trapped in a materialistic business all those years. I always felt that there was some big reason I was stuck there. But as much as I pleaded for an answer, I never knew what it was. Do you have any idea why I was there? Why I had to suffer so much?"

"No, my dear, I really don't, but I do believe that there is purpose in everything. All I can suggest is that you try to think back about why you chose to put yourself in that position. Remember what your thoughts, hopes, and dreams were. That is where you might find your answer."

# Chapter 10

These new ideas were very interesting, but all that thinking had totally exhausted me. As soon as I hit my bed, I fell asleep and had a dream so vivid it seemed real.

When I woke up the next morning, I couldn't wait to share my dream with Rose. "You're never going to believe it," I said to her breathlessly when I arrived in front of her bench. "I think I know why I was there!" She put up her hand as if to say, "Slow down there," and then she smiled with a look of anticipation.

After I sat down, I exclaimed again, "I think I know why I stayed in the company all that time. I had this amazing dream last night, and now it seems so clear."

I began to recount my dream for Rose. "I was back in my company talking to Celia, one of my employees, on the phone. She had been very unhappy at work. Talking a little bit longer, she let me know that her pent-up feelings were more than just frustrations at work. She was under a lot of stress, and a couple of people in her department had been constantly bickering with each other. Then, to make matters worse, someone close to her had died, and another member of her family was terribly ill.

"Rose, Celia was one of my favorite employees. She was always cheerful and fun to be with. In the dream, I was terribly sad as I could hear her heartache through the phone. By the time the call was over, we were both crying.

"The second I hung up the phone, it was as if there was a huge spotlight shining down on me from heaven. And in that moment, I suddenly knew . . . It was as if I was instantaneously shown why I was in the business. Rose, can you believe it? The question I have been asking myself over and over again was answered in an instant.

"In the dream, I was told, not in words but in a sudden knowing, that the business did not have anything at all to do with making products. The only purpose it served was a trumped-up reason for all those seemingly disconnected people to get together every day. And that each of us had something to give and to receive from every other person in the group. It was for that reason, and that reason alone, that the company existed.

"In the dream, I saw this big circle, like a wheel with many points of light on it, and every point represented someone who worked in my company. And I saw all these lines going out from each person to every other person on the wheel. There was all this connecting and interconnecting and intersecting of the lines. And the amazing thing was that I immediately knew what it all meant. Every person was there for a reason. Each one of us had a specific purpose for being there at that place and at that time with that group of people. We all thought we were there to produce a product, but in the dream, it was as if we had been drawn together for a higher purpose.

"It seemed as if this same principle could apply to all businesses, all groups, and all families, each representing their own circles. Rose," I exclaimed with excitement, "just imagine if the dream is true! What if the whole world operates in this perfect pattern that supports everything and everyone to their highest possible potential?

"The dream also made it clear to me that the company was not mine and Craig's but God's. And that I need not worry, for as long as it served its purpose, it would continue to exist. And when its purpose was complete, it would be gone. My only job was to show up every day and do what I do to the best of my ability. Rose, if we all really did have a reason for being there together, and I had known that at the time, can you imagine how different my life would have been? I was always convinced I was 100 percent responsible for everything and everyone, and that there was no escape. I always felt trapped, like I didn't have any choice in the matter.

"Anyway, as the dream ended, I was walking into the factory. My heart was light, and I was full of anticipation because, for the first time, I knew deep within me that something powerful, yet beyond my comprehension, was happening in that building with those particular people.

"Rose, I swear the dream was *so* real. This morning I feel like my entire perception about my company and all those years I spent there has changed! I haven't thought this deeply about the meaning of things in a very long time."

I sat there waiting for some reaction from Rose. When she hadn't spoken in some time, I looked over her way to find her smiling to herself.

Then I nudged her gently, asking in a whisper, "Do you think I'm going crazy?"

# Chapter 11

**M**y mind went back again to the memories of the previous year with the business and my personal life. The facts were becoming clearer as I sifted through them.

"Rose . . . now I'm thinking back to what was going on in my life. Craig was busy opening another location most of that year, so I was managing two factories and overseeing the office staff, as well. During that last year, several people started leaving the company, just one at a time, slowly. We were able to maintain, so I didn't hire new people to replace them. Until now, I had never really thought about it, but the crew was much smaller by the time I sold the business. So I suppose the dream I had kind of fits in with the fact that people left when their purpose for being there was fulfilled.

"But, Rose, there is even more to this. I remember something unusual that happened in the last few months I had the company. It was around the middle of June that I realized just how tenuous our financial situation was. Our vendors were going to stop the flow of supplies if they didn't get paid soon. It wasn't looking too promising, but I didn't want my employees to worry about their job security over their vacation. I had this big plan all worked out in my mind. If we did not get some additional funding by the middle of July, I would have to let some people go.

"But then suddenly, the last day of June, I strongly sensed I was supposed to let four people go that day. I had the strangest conviction about this, even though it went totally against 'The Plan.' All day I kept trying to bury this idea, but it would not let go of me. So at the end of the workday, I boarded the van carrying this specific group of people and let the ax fall. They were very upset, crying and asking me how I could do this to them.

"The next day was a Saturday, so no one would have

been at the factory, but I went over to check on a few things. I was standing on the production line, and all of a sudden it hit me. I was filled with remorse for what I had done. How could I have let these people go? How could I live without them in the company? Many of them were closer to me than my own husband by this time. I must have made a horrible mistake.

"In the very moment I had this thought, the phone rang. It was Celia, one of the people I had fired the day before. When I answered, she immediately started talking without letting me say another word. She was adamant, filled with conviction, as she almost commanded me, 'Angela, I wanted to call you to tell you that I know you did the exact right thing. Everything will be fine. We will all find jobs. I just know you did the right thing.'

"It seems like she hung up right after that. I remember being shocked at the time. It was uncanny how she had called at the exact minute I was doubting my decision."

I paused for a moment to gather my thoughts and then continued, "Rose, I think I'm beginning to understand a little bit more about what you have been sharing with me. I felt so alone, but now I see that I really wasn't. The answers had been there all along, but I was too blind to see—or possibly just too angry to notice.

"I remember the company's department heads. They took great pride in being able to solve problems without my help. The production supervisors were on the clock for at least an hour before I arrived every morning, mixing resin, checking color matches, making sure that all systems were running smoothly before the rest of the crew started to move forward with production.

"I recall one morning, as I walked over to check in with the pouring supervisor, she seemed irritated to see me coming in her direction. There was frustration in her tone as she blurted out, 'How is it that every morning when you come in, no matter where the problem is, you walk directly to that spot? How do you know that?'

"The fact is, Rose, I didn't know it. As far as I could see, I didn't have any reason to go to any particular place in the mornings. Her tone did give me a jolt, but I didn't have any explanation for her. I had no conscious memory of there being any special reason behind my early morning actions. Since I didn't see it for myself, I didn't give it any real thought at the time. The crew thought I had some kind of weird sixth sense or something.

"That was kind of odd, huh, Rose?"

"Hmm, not really." She paused for a moment and then continued, "Tell me, how did you feel about your employees?"

"They were the most wonderful, kindhearted, and dedicated people. They became like family to me."

"Did you take pride in the products of the company?"

"You know, I really did. We developed something that was unique in the marketplace, and the designs were beautiful."

"And how did you feel about your customers?"

"I was grateful that they did business with us and tried to give them the best possible product. In fact, we had a system on the line that required that everyone be vigilant for quality."

"So, that was your prayer, right?"

"Rose, I wasn't saying any prayers in those days. Mostly I was making demands when I communicated with God. I've told you, I was hostile."

I had been talking almost nonstop, but I could see she was a little bit disturbed. Sitting quietly now, she seemed to be searching for a way to get her point across. It seemed that there was nothing more important to her than helping me see what she knew was a profound truth. I sat there staring into space, happy to give my overworked brain a little rest.

After a few moments, even though she was still silent, I could see that her mood was becoming more hopeful. I glanced her way and noticed that she was nodding her head very slightly, this way and that, kind of like a student working a concept all the way through in her head before presenting it aloud.

Once again joyful, she asked, "Are you ready for some more questions?"

"Shoot!"

Happily, Rose continued on her quest. "Okay, about how many hours a day was your focus on your products, employees, and customers?"

"Almost every waking hour. At least twelve to sixteen hours every day."

"And how many hours per day would you say you spent 'venting'?"

"Well, just guessing? I'd say I spent about fifteen minutes lashing out and expressing my woes. That's about all the energy I had left after working such long hours."

I paused, once again reflecting on the pain I was able to pack into those sessions. Then I added, "So . . . . that would be one-fourth of an hour per day."

Another pause . . . "I get it. My focus was at least fifty to one on producing a good product versus yelling at God . . . Wow!"

I was shocked by this revelation. In my mind, I spent all my time being angry, but in reality, it was very little.

"I'm not really in tune with the prayer part here, but I sure understand the math. And if I go back to the idea of 'what you focus on expands,' I guess it really does ring true here."

"See, Angela, we are always praying. Our every thought, action, and attitude is telling God what we really want in our lives. Your life *is* your prayer!"

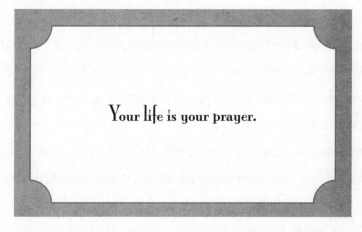

Your life is your prayer.

She pulled the card right out of her bag without even

looking. "Can't you see it? The life you lead, where you put your energy, is your most prevalent prayer. And certainly a life focused on producing the best products and caring for the welfare of your employees was a prayer that was continually answered. Everything you are telling me, about your employee calling you, about blindly going where the problems were . . . Well, they were both answers to the prayer that the largest part of your life had become.

"Your prayers were always being answered. You have always been taken care of. You just haven't been able to see it, because you did not realize you were getting exactly what you were asking for. Isn't it fascinating? I know it about knocked my socks off when I first realized it.

"In the case of you firing those people . . . well . . . isn't it interesting just how fast your prayer for help was answered? If it wasn't in God's perfect design, how would something like that ever happen? A fired employee calls her boss to tell her she knew she had done the right thing? See? The more energy, the more attention you put into anything, the more powerful connection there is to God's help. And you are never more than a breath away from it."

She sat there contented, her head tilted slightly upward,

gazing off into the late afternoon sky. She was there with me and a million miles away all at the same time. I was in awe of this woman sitting beside me, totally serene and radiating joy.

Just being with her, I felt awash with the strangest sense of quiet exhilaration. It was as if, at least for this instant, the past didn't matter, and I had no thought of the future. I was content to just be there in that moment. I felt peaceful, and that was something I had never really experienced. We sat in silence for a long while before she slowly came back from wherever her thoughts had taken her.

Patting my hand, she said, "Thank you for giving me such a wonderful day." I could see tears welling up in her eyes.

"Tomorrow, then?" she smiled as she rose to her feet.

Still feeling blissful and content just sitting there on that bench, I nodded slightly, adding, "I'll be here."

# Chapter 12

Later in the evening, I began thinking about the fact that I'd been without my car for over a week and had hardly missed it. In the past, being without wheels for even an hour would have made me feel trapped. Now my only thought was about how lucky I was that the stranger had shown up when he did. I was on the side of the road for only five minutes before he came to my rescue. And then for the tow truck driver to let my car sit on his lot until I could find the funds to get it fixed was really nice.

Considering the circumstances, it had worked out perfectly. I couldn't afford gas, anyway. Remembering the way

it all happened, I came to the conclusion that the car failures had been divine intervention. After all, if I'd been able
to leave, I never would have gotten to know the baglady.

As I was standing at the sink brushing my teeth before
bed, I looked up at the cards I'd taped to the bathroom
mirror. *Yes, Rose,* I thought to myself, *I can choose to see
things differently.*

The next morning, I woke up from a restful sleep feeling
energized. I had a great outlook for the day.

"Good morning," Rose said cheerfully as I took a seat
beside her on the now familiar bench.

"Rose," I said, suddenly serious, "thank you so much for
being patient with me and for taking the time to help me
see things differently. I'm stunned by how our talks have
altered my perception.

"Yesterday, you and I talked a lot about our relationship
with God. Something that has been on my mind is that,
even though I have been angry with God for so long, at the
same time I feel so guilty about it."

Taking my hands in hers, she whispered, "Oh, my dear,
you are his beloved child. Replace your guilt with love, and
all heaven rejoices.

"You know, Angela, it is really we who turn away from

God, not God from us. Every day, every moment, is a brand-new chance to see it differently. I personally think that the Creator is with us every step of the way. I've seen it so often in my own life that I just can't deny it. For me, it is the truth. There is not the smallest detail that escapes this truth. There is purpose in everything that crosses our path. Everything! It saddens me that, for the most part, people are blind to the impact of these seemingly small things. Can you imagine how fascinating the world would become if you could see the underpinnings of the divine plan? How each action or thought has a lasting effect on your life and the lives of those you touch? Certainly, you have read stories about how some chance occurrence changed a person's life forever.

"We tend to think that it is all about the big things and that so much is out of our hands. But there are no unimportant moments. None at all! Think about it for a minute. Let's just use a game of Solitaire as an example. You have one space free and two kings up. You choose to fill the space with one of the kings. The other one stays on a stack of cards. That one small move, that one small choice, changes the whole game. It could change whether you win or lose. It affects the amount of time the game will take.

The change in the game time changes everything about the rest of your day. You will have more or less time for other things. You can take the impact of that one king into eternity, because if you look deeply, you can see that the timing of the rest of your life is in some small way affected by that one move. And just think of the compounding effect of all the small moments and choices over a week's time— enough to affect an entire lifetime.

"Angela, the more you understand this, the more fascinating your life will be. Your understanding will change your life. You will stop seeing yourself as a victim of circumstances. Instead, you will see how much your thoughts and actions influence the world you see."

And with that, into her bag she plunged excitedly, looking for something else to share with me. Before long, she had it in her hand.

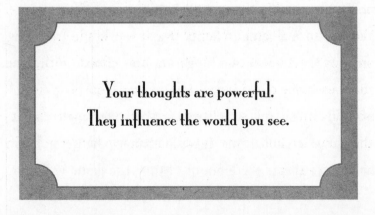

Your thoughts are powerful.
They influence the world you see.

She presented it to me as if it were the Hope Diamond. I read it, wrinkled up my face, and finally looked her way. She could read my look. *This little, old lady is crazy,* I thought.

Undaunted by my disbelief, the baglady continued, "Dear, maybe some example will come to you that will help you change your mind."

"Rose, I have a confession to make. Remember when we first met, and I told you I was leaving? Well, I already know that you were aware that I didn't go . . . "

She nodded in acknowledgement as I continued.

"Well, I tried to leave, but my car kept breaking down— twice in one day. Oh, Rose, it was a nightmare. First, my battery was drained. Then, when I finally got out of town, the whole car went dead right on the highway. I was so furious.

"But last night I thought back to all the circumstances of the breakdown, and I realized that it was kind of uncanny the way I was taken care of. My car just went dead right on the highway. I could have been stuck in the fast lane and possibly hit from behind, but I was able to maneuver it to the shoulder, and I was out of harm's way when it finally rolled to a stop.

"Right away, a man pulled off the road to help. And once he called for a tow truck, it seemed like the driver was there immediately. The driver was so consoling and helpful to keep the car on his lot and take me right to my front door. Oh, Rose, I was so unhappy about my plans being foiled that I'm afraid I was snippy with the driver, in spite of his being so helpful."

"Oh, Angela, we all mess up a lot until we finally see things as they really are. Take note of what you have done and learn from it. But no guilt or judgments, please. Feeling guilty for your own errors or having bad feelings toward others' shortcomings serves only to bind you to them. You have to let go of all that," she said in a serious tone.

Then, lightheartedly, arms waving cheerfully as if to wipe it all away, she exclaimed, "Any mistakes you made in the past, anything that went wrong yesterday . . . they count for nothing today. Every day is a new chance, a fresh start. It can be like a brand-new life. The hardest part of the whole process is to let go of the past.

"I know," she continued, "it's easier said than done." Feigning a serious, judgmental demeanor, she continued, "We get so set in our ways. The older we get, the worse it is. Sadly, many, many people, regardless of their level of success, are not really happy. So often, as we get older, we think we are so smart that our minds become closed to the very things that would set us free. We humans are a self-righteous lot sometimes," she giggled, quick to see the human condition clearly and yet with humor at the same time.

Rose paused for a moment, then immediately switched gears and was off on a different subject. "Oh, Angela, there is something I have been meaning to share with you. I think today would be a good day. Remember that story I gave you when we first met?"

With that, she pulled another copy of it out of the bag. Holding it reverently with her frail, little hands, she read it out loud to me.

Right before you were born, God placed in your right hand a brand-new artist's canvas, rolled up like a scroll. And in your left, a handful of brightly colored paints. He hugged you tightly and kissed you on the forehead. "Go into the world, my child, and make of your life a beautiful masterpiece."

Shocked at the sight of a newborn armed with such sophisticated materials, the doctor pried your little fingers from the gifts you were born with to your screams of protest.

"A baby cannot possibly have the skills to paint on canvas with oils."

Soon these gifts were replaced with a page outlined with soft blue lines, each with a number in it, and crayons labeled with matching numbers. As they tucked these in your crib, you were assured, "Life is about staying in the lines and painting by the numbers. If you do that, everything will work out fine."

And that is a lie!

—Author Unknown

After pausing a moment, she said, "Angela, the day I read that was the beginning of a whole new life for me. It impacted me so strongly that I immediately turned it over and wrote on the other side of it."

With that, she handed me the copy so I could read her note myself. It was written in 1978, thirty years ago.

I slowly read the note to myself.

May 23, 1978

Today, God sent an angel into my life with this story to remind me that I'm meant to be a masterpiece. All my life I've been surrounded, even at school as a child, by people who have told me to get in line and do what everyone else does. After many years of being told what to do and how to do it, I just got right in that line over and over again and forgot the canvas God gave me.

There has always been this nagging sense that something is amiss, but I've never been able to put my finger on it. From this day forward, I will paint my own unique masterpiece.

—Rose Kelley

"It took a long time for me to discover the things I'm sharing with you now," Rose continued, "but the point is that on that day, with all my heart, though I did not know it at the time, my prayer became to paint my masterpiece."

"Rose, what was your masterpiece?"

Laughing, she responded, "At first, I had no idea. I had to throw out all my judgments about what my life should be or the way things should work out. In fact, I pretty much threw out the word 'should' from my vocabulary. I became open to being shown the real meaning of my life. I wanted to understand the true nature of God. What did he really mean to impart to us? What did he want from us? How were we to be in this world?

"I had been pretty headstrong in my day, believing that I had the answers to everything. So much so that one of my friends emphatically informed me one day, 'Rose, you really do *not* have to be everyone's God.' Well, that took me aback for a minute until I realized that he had not really meant to insult me. In a way, he was right. I was always trying to take care of everything and everyone. And, quite frankly, it was wearing me out.

"He had a twinkle in his eye as he continued good-naturedly, 'Do you realize that the sun rises and sets every day without your help? Grass grows, seasons turn . . . Why do you feel so responsible for everything?'

"It took me awhile, but from those words, I finally learned to relax a little bit. Eventually, I learned to follow my heart, wherever it led me, and I stopped worrying about my future. I walked out into the world empty, willing to be filled. And, most important, I was finally allowing God to be in charge. After all, he does do a pretty good job with the sun, grass, and stars," she laughed.

"I was astounded by the changes that occurred in my life at that time. And I'm delighted by the things I get to be a part of these days. What a wonderful life I have." With that, her mind again wandered away from me. By now I knew not to worry. She would be back in her own time. It was such an amazing day. Just being there, sitting on the bench and enjoying the smell of spring was good enough for me.

Rose startled me with her sudden excitement as she began going through that bag again. With her head in her bag, she was totally preoccupied, while a sudden panic welled up in me. All these little stories and sayings were fine for her, but I had real-world problems. Like, how am I going to survive this next week? I touched her arm, trying to get her to pry her head out of the bag and talk turkey with me.

"Rose," I pleaded, trying to get her attention, "when I am with you, it seems like everything is easy. Sitting on this bench, I somehow forget about my problems, but the rest of my life is still in shambles. I feel so alone and scared. I don't have any idea how I am going to eat next week or get my car back."

Just as I finished speaking, her head resurfaced out of the bag. Pleased with her find, she smiled at me with no reaction to my concerns.

"Rose," I said more forcefully, "I'm drowning here. What am I going to do?"

With that, she proudly presented me with another card. She turned to face me, and two fingers from each hand held the card right under her chin, just as a child might present her latest finger painting for approval.

Let go and let God.

I just shook my head, exasperated with her childlike faith. She didn't have any answers for me, after all. She'd just gotten old and feebleminded. "Let go and let God" is good in theory, but it certainly is not the answer for my wretched life.

But she seemed so happy, and I didn't want to burst her bubble. I dutifully took the card she handed me, made some excuse to leave, and moped all the way home.

# Chapter 13

The last few days had been a roller coaster. I had experienced moments of bliss while sitting with Rose in the peaceful little world she created, but my reality kept crashing back in. The last thing I needed now was one more betrayal, but it was waiting for me in the mailbox. Perfect—threat of a lawsuit right there in big, bold print. And now the credit-card companies were starting to close in on me. Nameless collection agents were stalking me. Then there was my ex-husband, who managed to weasel his way out of the IRS problems on a technicality, and the furious landlords who would never receive their lease payments. I hated them all.

*The baglady has simply not been taking my massive problems seriously. Her little slogans cannot fix my life. There has got to be something in that bag of hers more powerful than that. Today, I will try harder to get her to listen to me and focus on the real issues at hand.*

"Rose," I said as I sat down beside her, "I am so filled with anger that I can't see straight. It feels like the whole world is conspiring to bring me down. I think you are the only person I know that I do not hate right now."

"Oh, Angela, don't even say such a thing." With that, she clasped her hands to her ears as if the words themselves caused her head to hurt.

I was shocked by her dramatics. Always before, anything I said, no matter how harsh, had met with her easy acceptance. Why was she having such a strong reaction today? I think she was saying some kind of prayer under her breath; her eyes were closed, and she had a pained look on her face.

She seemed to console herself, and then her gentle nature returned. When she looked at me again, kindness but also pity filled her eyes.

"Rose, what did I say that upset you so much?"

The Baglady's Guide to Elegant Living

"Oh, Angela," she pleaded, "please do not let hatred and judgments overtake you. The only person you are hurting is yourself. Everyone, no matter what the situation looks like, is always doing the best they can."

And with that, I could see tears well up in her eyes. Rose appeared to be holding some deep sadness that she didn't want to share. She took the hanky that was stuffed in her watchband and dabbed the sides of her eyes. I was stunned by how deeply my words had affected her.

Somehow, I knew not to speak. It was my time to just sit with her for a change. After a while, she reached slowly for her bag and looked through her papers thoughtfully, without any effort to speak.

She must have found what she was looking for as she pulled out a page and held it on her lap, but she made no move to give it to me. Her eyes were cast down for a few moments; she seemed to be refreshing her memory of everything the page contained. She was so thoughtful, the way she sat there; it was as if she were in communion with something much bigger than herself.

"Angela, several years ago I read a book by a Buddhist monk, Thich Nhat Hanh. When I started it, I could see lots of unfairness in the world. In my opinion then, the world would do very well without some people and some things. I could not see the importance of the whole, the "everything" that God had designed. As I read this book, though, I realized that the dark and the light are two sides of the same coin. And that one without the other simply doesn't work. May I read you my favorite poem from the book?"

It was so important to her. I nodded and gave her my full attention.

She read it slowly, with much reverence.

## Please Call Me by My True Names

Do not say that I'll depart tomorrow
because even today I still arrive.

Look deeply: I arrive in every second
to be a bud on a spring branch,
to be a tiny bird, with wings still fragile,
learning to sing in my new nest,
to be a caterpillar in the heart of a flower,
to be a jewel hiding itself in a stone.

I still arrive, in order to laugh and to cry,
in order to fear and to hope.
The rhythm of my heart is the birth and
death of all that are alive.

I am the mayfly metamorphosing
on the surface of the river,
and I am the bird which, when spring comes,
arrives in time to eat the mayfly.

I am the frog swimming happily in the clear pond,
and I am also the grass snake who,
approaching in silence, feeds itself on the frog.

I am the child in Uganda, all skin and bones,
my legs as thin as bamboo sticks,
and I am the arms merchant,
selling deadly weapons to Uganda.

I am the twelve-year-old girl, refugee on a small boat,
who throws herself into the ocean
after being raped by a sea pirate,
and I am the pirate, my heart not yet capable
of seeing and loving.

I am a member of the politburo,

with plenty of power in my hands,

and I am the man who has to pay

his "debt of blood" to my people,

dying slowly in a forced labor camp.


My joy is like spring,

so warm it makes flowers bloom in all walks of life.

My pain is like a river of tears,

so full it fills the four oceans.


Please call me by my true names,

so I can hear all my cries and laughs at once,

so that I can see that my joy and pain are one.


Please call me by my true names,

so I can wake up,

and so the door of my heart can be left open,

the door of compassion.

—Thich Nhat Hanh

There was a long silence as she finished. Rose seemed to have left this world as she read it. I wanted to pay attention to the poem, but I was so overwhelmed by her transformation that it took most of my attention.

It seemed to me that she existed within the whole of it.

# Chapter 14

I took the strange poem home that night, determined to figure out what could have such a profound effect on Rose.

I reread it several times. *Can she really see herself in every part of this poem? As a starving child? A rapist? A killer? Certainly, I must be missing something.* It was beyond my comprehension.

The next morning, I sat down next to her, poem in hand. "Rose, what is it about that poem that affects you so deeply?" I asked sincerely. "Tell me what it really means to you."

Rose smiled serenely before replying. "To me, it speaks

about forgiveness and compassion. For example, the sea pirate had never been taught to love. And though his actions were despicable, how miserable must his life be that he has no caring for another. In your life, many people have hurt you, but what fear or emptiness deep inside would lead them to decide to harm another? Find it in yourself to have compassion, my dear, and your anger and hatred will be transformed. When you have learned to forgive others, then so will you be able to forgive yourself and realize that everyone is always doing the best they can. See that truth and you will, as a result, become free to truly love.

"Do you remember what Jesus said as he was hanging on the cross? He wasn't angry and filled with hatred for those who caused him to suffer. He was filled with compassion, even in his anguish. 'Forgive them, Father, for they know not what they do.'

"He was filled with compassion, for he alone understood how much their actions were hurting them. I think he also meant, 'Forgive them for they know not what they are doing to themselves when they seek to harm another.' You see, Angela, you will reap what you sow. When you hate, you diminish your own life. You live in darkness. And when you truly can view others in the world with compassion, all heaven rejoices.

"Instead of seeing the perfection in all aspects of life, we humans are always judging. Think about it, Angela. We decide that some things are good, others bad. We don't take time to see that without both the good and the bad, the dirty and the clean, our world would be nothing. Take a rose, for instance. Many people would consider it the most beautiful and highly revered of all flowers, a symbol of love and commitment. And yet, where does a rose come from? It rises up from the dirt. And what happens to a rose after its bloom is past? In a few short days, it goes from being the focus of delight to just another piece of trash to be thrown out in the garbage.

"And through the process of decay, the garbage becomes earth that feeds the plant, so it can bring forth another rose. It is the circle of life in all its messy glory.

"We do not always see the reason that things turn out the way they do, but if you can trust in the great design, then you will be able to suspend judgment. And you must suspend judgment in order to find true contentment and peace within."

Rose suddenly became very animated and excitedly reached for her bag. "Oh, Angela, I have the most wonderful story for you! Have you ever read *The Rabbi's Gift*? I know I have a copy in here somewhere. It is one of my favorites!"

Papers and cards were spewing out as she dug deeply into her bag. I jumped up to catch them before the wind scattered them. She looked like a character out of the comics. It was funny to watch her reckless abandon as she searched for her treasure.

I wanted to stop her and get her to talk to me about my *real* problems. She seemed to have so much wisdom, maybe she could be of some value to me if I could just shake her into reality for a few minutes. But, alas, she was too tied up in her made-up world to get serious about my problems.

Just then, she stood up straight, tipping the bag and the rest of the contents on the ground. "*Eureka!*" she hooted. "I found it! This is such a lark, Angela. You are really going to love it," she shouted with glee.

*I'm about to run out of food, and this little, old lady is trying to fix my life with fairy tales and slogans.* I took a deep breath and let out a sigh, accepting the story she was offering me. *Maybe tomorrow we can talk about something important.*

# Chapter 15

I couldn't figure out why Rose carried around that big bag of . . . what? Happy little thoughts? And she seemed to put so much stock in them. To her those mementos seemed more precious than gold. And it was sure clear that she thought the things in that bag were the wisdom that could fix whatever ailed me.

*I've got news for her. The papers in that sack don't even remotely resemble what I need right now. The only paper that's going to do me any good would be a rolled-up wad of hundred-dollar bills.*

I laid the story down on the table when I got home and

went out for a run. For some reason, our latest conversation was irritating me. I had hoped I could work my frustrations out on the pavement, but my mind was on a rampage that wouldn't stop.

*Just when I take a step forward and think we are on the edge of some kind of answer for me, she throws out something new from her bag, and I feel like I'm still miles away from any kind of solution. What am I going to have to do to get her to listen to me?*

I finally got some peace after I decided that I just wasn't going to read *The Rabbi's Gift*. Upon arriving back home, I grabbed a quick bite, tossed the baglady's story in the kitchen trash can, and flipped on the TV.

I was cleaning up the dishes a couple of hours later, pulling the basket of grounds out of the coffeemaker to set it up for morning. Leaning over the trash can, I saw the story there on top of the pile.

With a sigh of exasperation, I pulled the story out before dumping the coffee grounds in, sat on the couch, and read it.

## The Rabbi's Gift

A monastery had fallen upon hard times. Once a great order, as a result of waves of antimonastic persecution in the seventeenth and eighteenth centuries and the rise of secularism in the nineteenth, all its branch houses were lost, and it had become decimated to the extent that there were only five monks left in the decaying mother house: the abbot and four others, all over seventy in age. Clearly, it was a dying order.

In the deep woods surrounding the monastery there was a little hut that a rabbi from a nearby town occasionally used for a hermitage. Through their many years of prayer and meditation, the old monks had become a bit psychic, so they could always sense when the rabbi was in his hermitage. "The rabbi is in the woods. The rabbi is in the woods again," they would whisper to each other. As he agonized over the imminent death of his order, it occurred to the abbot at one such time to visit the hermitage and ask the rabbi if, by some possible chance, he could offer any advice that might save the monastery.

The rabbi welcomed the abbot at his hut. But when the abbot explained the purpose of his visit, the rabbi could only commiserate with him. "I know how it is," he exclaimed. "The spirit has gone out of the people. It is the same in my town. Almost no one comes to the synagogue anymore." So the old abbot and the old rabbi wept together. Then they read parts of the Torah and spoke of deep things. The time came when the abbot had to leave. They embraced each other. "It has been a wonderful thing that we should meet after all these years," the abbot said, "but I still failed in my purpose for coming here. Is there nothing you can tell me? No piece of advice you can give me that would help me save my dying order?"

"No, I am sorry," the rabbi responded. "I have no advice to give. The only thing I can tell you is that the Messiah is one of you."

When the abbot returned to the monastery, his fellow monks gathered around him to ask, "Well, what did the rabbi say?"

"He couldn't help," the abbot answered. "We just wept and read the Torah together. The only thing he did say, just as I was leaving—it was something cryptic—was that the Messiah is one of us. I don't know what he meant."

In the days and weeks and months that followed, the old monks pondered this and wondered whether there was any possible significance to the rabbi's words.

The Messiah is one of us? Could he possibly have meant one of us monks here at the monastery? If that's the case, which one? Could it be the abbot? Yes, if he meant anyone, he probably meant Father Abbot. He has been our leader for more than a generation. On the other hand, he might have meant Brother Thomas. Certainly Brother Thomas is a holy man. Everyone knows that Thomas is a man of light. Certainly he could not have meant Brother Elred!

Elred gets crotchety at times. But, come to think of it, even though he is a thorn in people's sides, when you look back on it, Elred is virtually always right. Often very right. Maybe the rabbi did mean Brother Elred. But surely not Brother Phillip. Phillip is so passive, a real nobody. But then, almost mysteriously, he has a gift for somehow always being there when you need him. He just magically appears by your side. Maybe Phillip is the Messiah.

Of course, the rabbi didn't mean me. He couldn't possibly have meant me. I'm just an ordinary person. Yet, supposing he did? Suppose I am the Messiah? Oh, God, not me. I couldn't be that much for you, could I?

As they contemplated in this manner, the old monks began to treat each other with extraordinary respect on the off chance that one among them might be the Messiah. And, on the off chance that each monk himself might be the Messiah, they began to treat themselves with extraordinary respect.

Because the forest in which it was situated was beautiful, it so happened that people occasionally came to visit the monastery to picnic on its tiny lawn, to wander along some of its paths, even now and then to go into the dilapidated chapel to meditate. As they did so, even without being conscious of it, they sensed this aura of extraordinary respect that now began to surround the five old monks and seemed to radiate out from them and permeate the atmosphere of the place.

There was something strangely attractive, even compelling, about it. Hardly knowing why, they began to come back to the monastery more frequently to picnic, to play, and to pray. They began to bring their friends to show them this special place. And their friends brought their friends.

Then it happened that some of the younger men who came to visit the monastery started to talk more and more with the old monks. After a while, one asked if he could join them. Then another. And another. So, within a few years, the monastery once again became a thriving order and, thanks to the rabbi's gift, a vibrant center of light and spirituality in the realm.

—Author Unknown

*"The Rabbi's Gift" as it appears in M. Scott Peck's Prologue from* The Different Drum. *Reprinted with permission of Simon & Schuster Adult Publishing Group, 1987.*

As much as I had not wanted to read it, I couldn't help but admit that it did have a good message. Oh . . . if life could only be that easy. The monastery was revived and flourished all because the monks considered the possibility that one of them could be the Messiah. I wonder what the rabbi really meant? Certainly, he wasn't actually saying that one of the monks was the Messiah.

The next morning, when the bench was in sight, a moment of dread struck me. Rose was missing. Since the day we met, I could always find her there. I talked myself into calming down and decided to sit and wait for her. Before I knew it, an hour had elapsed.

Just as I started to panic, a sudden gust of wind came up. I closed my eyes momentarily to protect them from the dust in the air, and when I opened them again, there on my lap was one of her famous index cards. I immediately looked around, but the baglady was nowhere to be found. *She is certainly a mysterious woman.*

I was beginning to get used to her ways, so I soon settled back on the bench and read the card.

> Everything in the entire world is God's.
> All people, all places, all things at all times belong entirely to God.
> Practice believing it.

I had to laugh. It was so bizarre and yet so funny that her wisdom could be delivered even in her absence.

After sitting there a few more minutes pondering the rabbi, the monks, and the newest index card, I decided to treat myself to some comfort food—lunch at McDonald's. It was a little bit of a walk, but with the whole day ahead of me, I had time.

I hit McDonald's right at noon, and both the drive-through and the inside lines were already backed up. My jaw tightened; I was slightly irritated that the service would be delayed. As I was standing there, frozen in a line of customers that wasn't going anywhere, I watched a mom in the parking lot unload five little kids from a car. They were dressed identically in red T-shirts, blue jeans, and white sneakers, each holding the next one's hand. They looked like a string of paper dolls crossing to the door. Glancing down at the latest index card still in my hand, it was easy to see that they were God's kids. They were so well behaved. The mom was God's, too. The line dragged on, barely moving. The lobby was packed. I let out a big sigh; my tension rose.

By the time I made it to the counter, I had forgotten that God had anything to do with McDonald's. My demeanor was curt as I ordered. When my number was finally called to pick up my food, it was evident by the tears so close to falling from the server's eyes that I wasn't the only one who had forgotten that she was God's. With a few kind words, a smile, and a quick exchange of receipt for food, I walked away from the counter.

Thankful to finally have my food, I sat in the dining room, eating without further delay. When it came time to leave, I gathered up my tray to dump the trash on my way out, only to notice that the slow-up at the counter was not the only problem they were having that day. The trash bins were overflowing, and people had resorted to just leaving everything on the tables. Seeing that, I normally would not have worried about following suit. But it wasn't any ordinary day at McDonald's. Today, it was God's dining room. And today, it mattered a lot. I waited for the bags to be emptied. After dumping my own trash, I cleaned up the trays that had been left on the table next to me.

Sitting in the park after lunch, I looked at the world around me. The trees, the birds, the picnic tables—they were all God's. They were the best trees, birds, and picnic tables I had ever seen in my life.

# Chapter 16

As I approached our bench the next day, I was eager to share with Rose all that had taken place since our last visit, so I quickly sat down beside her. "Rose," I said, breathless with excitement about my discovery, "who would ever think that a simple trip to McDonald's could have such a profound effect on me?"

"What do you mean, my dear?"

"Well, you know that card that so mysteriously landed in my lap yesterday?" I looked at her to reinforce that I knew she had a hand in it somehow. "Well, yesterday, when I was at McDonald's, it really sunk in. I mean, I really got it!

"I practiced seeing *everything* as God's. And, Rose, it made such a huge difference in my perception, a huge difference in the way I felt about everything I came in contact with. It was night and day. What an amazing concept. Now I can see how the monastery changed. With the word 'everything' in my mind, I could not make a distinction. I mean, I didn't have the latitude to pick and choose what belonged to God and what did not. That really struck a chord with me and helped it sink in.

"When you read that poem to me . . . you know the one with the arms merchant and the sea pirate? Well, I couldn't imagine anyone who could have compassion for them. But now I see, even though they may be lost . . . how did you say it? That they turned away from God? Well, according to the Bible, *The Rabbi's Gift*, and your poem, once you break it down . . . well, they are part of the everything that is God's! The very breath they breathe is thanks to God.

"I gotta be honest with you and tell you that I really do not get why God allows them to live, but I can see the profound truth of it. And, for right now, that is good enough for me. I'm just excited that I can see it."

She was delighted with my report, beaming ear to ear. "Well, then," she exclaimed, "today we must do something special to celebrate." With that, Rose took a quick look around, seeming to search for something in the park. Soon, she was pointing off to the right of us. "Angela, do you see that little wooden box over there by the oak tree? Would you be a darling and bring it over here for me?"

As I was returning, I watched in amazement as she pulled a starched linen luncheon cloth edged with embroidered lace out of her bag. With the flair of a waiter in a fine restaurant, she snapped it open, letting it drift down over the crate. Continuing with finesse, she waved her hand, open-palmed, through the air and presented me with her table. Another movement invited me to sit. Back into the bag again, she emerged with two bone-china teacups and matching saucers. They were delicately hand-painted with a flurry of violets. Last to be delivered from the bag was a white fluted pouring Thermos of herbal tea. As she filled our cups with all the impeccable etiquette one would expect at the Russian Tea Room, she inquired, "Sugar?"

"Oh, yes, I believe I will," I responded with equal sophistication, smiling all the while. With that, she reached in that same bag and pulled out a lovely, little antique sugar bowl and an ornate silver sugar spoon. Pinkies extended, together we sipped tea in our cozy, makeshift bistro, under a canopy of fluorescent green leaves. Natural and expansive arrangements of planted redbuds and dogwoods surrounded us. As we chatted about the weather, the whole setup seemed surreal, and I wasn't convinced it was really happening.

When we were done, as she was putting away the tea things, I commented on how she always seemed to be able to pull whatever was needed out of her bag at a moment's notice. She just smiled, making a little chirping sound as she shrugged and finished her work.

"That was so much fun!" she said as she brushed off her skirt and set her bag off to one side. "Now, what shall we talk about today?"

"Let's talk about your bag," I chided, knowing she had no intention of sharing.

"Another day, perhaps!" she said, eyes twinkling. The wisdom of her age and her zest for life had given her timeless beauty and radiance. Rose's softly wrinkled skin was exquisite in the same way of the age-cracked sugar bowl and weathered silver spoon from her bag.

Still today, I carry that picture in my mind, whenever I think of her.

# Chapter 17

**M**oments later, my cell phone rang. The caller ID brought me back to reality in an instant. That particular bill collector had been threatening me in a similar fashion to those I'd witnessed in gangster movies. It wasn't like he was going to have me eliminated, but he did seem to regard my inability to pay as a crime worthy of the death penalty.

I was paralyzed at the thought of having to talk to him again. Finally, the phone stopped ringing. Having been jerked back to reality and my imminent problems, I started out slowly.

"Rose, I'm truly grateful for what I learned at McDonald's. And I can see that you have a lot of wisdom about some things. I mean, you see the big picture in such a powerful way. But I'm really scared. I don't think you understand that my needs are urgent . . . and personal. I appreciate you helping me change my worldview, but I am in a desperate situation."

As usual, and as if she hadn't heard a word I said, she broke in with enthusiasm. "Oh, Angela, I heard the most wonderful story last night. I know it was meant for you.

"You see, there was a young Indian brave who had just passed the test to become a warrior. He would join the other men in his first battle to protect the tribe. Even at that, he had his misgivings. He went to the chief and talked with him, saying, 'I am proud to be going into my first battle to defend our honor and my people. But it is like I have two wolves fighting in my head. The black one is my fear for the battle ahead, and the white one is fierce and brave, ready to defend our people. There is so much fighting in my head that it is making me crazy. Please, can you tell me which wolf will win?'

"The chief did not hesitate for even a moment before he stated emphatically, 'The white wolf will win.'

"Puzzled by the chief's confidence in light of this terrible conflict, the brave asked, 'How do you know this?'"

"Again, the chief was steadfast in his sureness of the result. 'Because you will feed the white one.'"

Rose was excited as she continued, "That is such a perfect story about life. You can either be overcome by fear, or you can turn your back on it and focus your mind in a more empowering way. Don't you see? That is what you must do in order to move forward."

In contrast to her commitment to conveying the message of the story, I immediately noticed a change in her demeanor. In the silence of those few moments, she moved back to her overwhelming gentleness that I had initially grown accustomed to and had been missing lately.

Then she turned toward me, took both my hands in hers, and looked at me with such compassion that it almost made me cry.

Quietly, she started, "My dear, over the last several days, you have been feeling very agitated with me, haven't you?"

Uh-oh. The tears were coming now, and I couldn't stop them. I broke her grasp to grab a tissue out of my pocket. In the few minutes I took to compose myself, she seemed to freeze-frame in that pose, hands held open for me, eyes expressing complete acceptance. She didn't move a muscle.

At last, when I had collected myself and placed my hands back in hers, she was immediately back in animation mode.

Again, slowly, sweetly, she started to talk. "You think I haven't heard you. You think I don't see how much you are hurting, how scared you are." They were statements and yet questions at the same time.

I nodded through tears that were starting up again.

"But I do. I know you feel lost and lonely and hundreds of other emotions that are separating you from life. This is affecting you so much that you can't see the light at the end of the tunnel." She paused and then nodded her head while repeating, "I know . . . I know. If you could pretend for a moment that you are the Indian brave, and I am the chief, I would only say that I am teaching you how to feed the white wolf. Only by feeding what is powerful inside you will you learn how to be in this world."

She could see I was shivering, as much from the chilly spring morning as from the crying and flood of emotions running through my body. Rose reached into her bag and pulled out a pale green chenille throw. It was as warm as if it had been pulled directly out of the dryer as she wrapped it around me. I was instantly comforted. A sense of peace shot through to my bones. Stunned, I looked at her with surprise and amazement. How could this fuzzy old blanket that had been in that bag for at least several hours be so warm?

She didn't give me much time to think about it. Having my physical needs now met, she continued. And this time, like the warmth wrapped around me, the truth of her words began to sink in.

The baglady was reverent as she continued, almost as if she were imparting to me a great secret that no one else was privy to. "Angela, when your heart is filled with love, every cell filled with love, your fears will fade away. And as you give up your judgments of what is right or fair, your eyes will be opened in a new way. You were able to experience just the slightest glimpse of that feeling yesterday at McDonald's, and later at the park."

I was still somewhat shaken, and though I wanted so desperately to understand, Rose was way over my head with her lofty love talk. Noticing my look of confusion, she took my hands in hers and began to speak more softly. "I'm going to sit here with you. Close your eyes, dear. Now I want you to think back to yesterday. Remember how you felt sitting at the park? Remember the perfection you felt?

How you could see that all things were God's?"

Pausing for a few minutes, allowing me time to settle into stillness, she then continued slowly, "Do you feel it? Are you there yet?"

I nodded. I was there. Enjoying the sunshine, the trees. Then tears began to flow. Not from sadness or fear. I couldn't understand why.

Rose whispered to me as she handed me a linen handkerchief, "It's okay. Just be with it. I'm here. There is no hurry. Breathe it all in. Notice everything."

I don't know how much time passed as we sat there. Things that I never even noticed yesterday came to my attention as I relaxed into the memory. After a while, with water still leaking uncontrollably from my closed eyes, I asked out loud, "Why am I crying? This is crazy."

"What are you feeling?"

Her question took me aback. "Well," I whispered, "I'm in awe of the enormity of God." I paused again. "For each of the things I am experiencing, remembering the trees, the sky . . . I feel grateful. Rose, I mean really grateful. It's like I am overwhelmed by it. Yeah, that's it!" I said, as I opened my eyes. "Overwhelming gratitude. I've never experienced anything like that before."

"Ah, yes, gratitude!" she chirped. "Angela, gratitude is one of the main ingredients of true happiness." With that she reached again into her bag, presented me with a silver package tied up with metallic gold ribbon, and motioned me to open it. When I removed the wrapping, I saw that it was a beautiful, hardbound journal.

She smiled as her eyes met mine. Then, attempting to take on the demeanor of an Indian chief, she sat up straight and proud. With a serious look on her face she spoke. "This journal will help you feed the white wolf."

Then leaving that moment behind, and again becoming her cheerful self, she added, "You know, Angela, writing down some things you feel grateful for each day will be a good way to start." She hesitated for a moment and then added, "Oh, yes, there will still be the crazy talk in your head that can pull you back into worry and regret, but gratitude will bring you back to a loving state time and time again. We are human, after all," she giggled.

"I'm human, but I'm not so sure about you," I laughed, as I whisked the throw off with fanfare and wrapped it around the baglady, hugging her as I did.

The sun was already low in the sky as we got up to leave. It had been quite a day—the tea party, the emotional roller coaster, and the myriad of things that came out of that bag. Even though I knew there was a lot to learn, at last I felt that the baglady really understood what I needed. Her teaching methods still did not make a lot of sense to me, but I had a feeling that we were moving in a positive direction. That, at least, gave me some comfort.

# Chapter 18

Walking home, with the journal in hand, I made a real effort to look at the circumstances of my life from a different perspective. As I walked, I made a commitment to myself that I would find four things for which I was truly grateful before turning in for the evening.

I got home, grabbed a pencil, and numbered the first page. Number one was actually easy. I wrote down "The baglady" in bold print at the top of the page. As I sat there, I recalled sweet memories of our first meeting, her unique personality, the love she exuded, her upbeat attitude.

Every thought of her made me smile. She was a complete delight, like a geriatric Mary Poppins.

Number two. *What else am I grateful for?* My good health. Yes, thank God I am physically strong, a picture of good health.

Number three . . . *Hmm.* I thought about my desperate financial situation, an absolute downer. *But no, I must keep it positive.* I started running around the loft, looking into any place I thought I might have some change or a few dollars stashed away. After a few minutes, I made a game out of it. In a surprising turn of events, I found a $100 bill under the lining of one of my dress shoes. (I used to hide money in my dress shoes when I traveled.) And by the time I counted the change in the jar and had corralled dollars from my purse and pockets, I had a lot more money than I had thought. At this point in my life, $158.32 was a small fortune.

So number three was $158.32. *I'm grateful for my found money.* Shoot, that one made my day. Things weren't as bad as I thought. By the time I had written down the money, I was in a great mood. After all, that was enough money to get me through another two weeks if I was frugal. I had been multitasking, and the buzzer on the microwave indicated that my frozen dinner was ready. I decided to celebrate my good fortune. I lit some candles, turned the lights down low, put on my favorite CD, and leisurely ate dinner, savoring my newfound wealth with a backdrop of soft, melodic sounds drifting through the loft.

I played the CD again and decided to snuggle into my bed early that evening to reflect on the day and think more about number four. There was a full moon splashing a silvery blue light in the window and across my bed. That beautiful luminescent orb seemed to be shining just for me. Number four: the moon shining in on me.

For the longest time, I lay there mesmerized by the light of the moon. Holding Rose's gift close to my chest, I fell into a peaceful sleep and had the most unusual dream.

I'm in a compound where all the buildings are made of cement blocks. I'm sitting on a porch visiting with several other people. All of a sudden, two humanlike creatures with big, soulful eyes walk around the corner of the building. I think they are from another planet, but they look harmless, and none of us on the porch are the least bit concerned. They walk up and sit on the porch with us. They exude kindness. One of them looks at me as he begins trying to communicate in a sign language. He touches his heart, then crosses both hands across his chest, and slowly opens one arm out to me. He does this several times, each time very slowly and deliberately in gentle movements. I know he is saying "I love you." He wants me to do it back to him. So I think, oh well, what could it hurt? At the same measured speed as he did, I touch my heart, then fold my arms across my chest and slowly unfold my arm out in a gesture to him.

The second my outstretched arm is pointed at his heart, I am filled with a blissful feeling. It feels almost like electricity entering my fingers. At the same time I feel the sensation hit my hand, the feeling moves through my entire body. And suddenly, instantaneously, the most important truths are imparted to me, and in such a profound way that every worry I have about anything is immediately erased from my consciousness. I'm euphoric.

Shortly after that, streams of people start pouring into the compound. Everyone is afraid, and they are all congregating at the church. I walk down to see what is going on and find out that another country has declared war on the United States. They are starting to invade our borders, and the people are scared to death.

When I get to the church, I sit in the front row. While everyone else is afraid, I am still totally blissful. I alone know that nothing bad can happen to us, if we learn and practice the truths. The preacher is very solemn and serious. He speaks for a few minutes, and then he asks the audience if anyone knows what protects us in troubling times like these.

Everyone else is cowering in silence, and I am sitting in the front row, waving my arm back and forth excitedly, repeating, "I know. I know!" The preacher motions me to come up and tell the congregation.

So I get up and, walking back and forth across the stage, I exclaim with enthusiasm, "It's peace, it's love, it's forgiveness, it's gratitude, and it is acceptance." I have such conviction in my belief that nothing can shake it. I am absolutely sure that these values are the key to everything.

When I woke up, I remembered the dream vividly, and I still felt energized by it. Peace, love, forgiveness, gratitude, and acceptance. How interesting that these were the very things that Rose had been talking to me about. When I thought about it, all her stories and slogans related to these things in one way or another. I recognized these as good values, but I still didn't understand how they would help me out of my current situation.

# Chapter 19

I could hardly wait to tell Rose about my evening and the dream. I sat down beside her and handed her my journal, opened to the first page.

"Rose, you are going to be so proud of me," I giggled. "See there! I found four things to be grateful for, even in my pathetic life." I laughed out loud. "Holy smokes, Rose, I found $100 in my shoe last night. I'm in the money! Can you believe that?"

She nodded her head at me. "Well, Angela, as a matter of fact, I can. Remember way back when, I told you what you focus on expands. You were focused on the good things in your life, and more good came to you!" With that, she joined in the laughter. She was giddy with delight. I had a fleeting thought that she and I were laughing—but for two different reasons. But never mind that, I had to tell her about my dream.

I continued, "You will never believe the dream I had last night." I recounted the dream as the baglady listened intently to every detail.

As I finished, I turned to her and questioned, "Rose, do you see it? That dream follows right along with all the stories and little sayings you've been giving me. They are lofty ideals, no doubt about it. But . . . well . . ." I continued with hesitation, "I just don't see how they will help me out of my current situation. And the way I figure it, I've only got about two weeks to come up with some serious answers."

Anxiously, I continued, "Yesterday, you assured me that you did recognize the bind I'm in. So today I'm begging you. Please tell me. How can I fix my life? What do I have to do? I'm ready to listen. But you have to put me on the fast track. Okay?"

"Ooh . . . kay!" She drew out the word as if debating whether or not I really meant it. "But you may be quite surprised with what I show you."

Starting again, she queried, "Will you make a deal to suspend your judgments and . . ."

"Scout's honor," I swore as I raised my hand in the salute before she could even finish her sentence.

She laughed at my enthusiasm and then scolded me goodnaturedly, "Wait just a minute, Angela. I'm really serious about this. I want you to take a little time to consider your decision. This may not be all that easy." Then she looked at me cheerfully and added, "I might just turn your world upside down!"

"Okay," I apologized, "I'll be quiet and listen to your proposal."

Taking on the demeanor of a serious-minded professor, she said, "Okay, I'll start over. Will you suspend your judgments and beliefs about the way you think life works . . . just for the next week . . . and be open to looking at it from an entirely different perspective? If you are willing, we can make a lot of progress. I'm certain you will discover some things that will help you.

"I'll assign homework, and you must do everything in your power to focus on grasping these new concepts," she cautioned. "At the end of the week, you are free to go back to your old way of thinking . . . if that is what you choose."

From the first day I met her, Rose seemed to have a beautiful but naive way of looking at the world. Everything was so easy for her. She always seemed so unassuming and yet gently endeavored to help me see the positive side of things. I was willing to invest a week. After all, I had no other plan.

"Rose," I said thoughtfully, "I really am ready to listen, to have you help me understand the way you see things. I know I have been a very reluctant student so far. Hardheaded might be a better term," I confessed as I smiled in her direction. "But I seriously do want you to teach me what you know. Really."

This time, Rose was thrilled to hear my answer. She was as excited as if I'd given her a million dollars. "Oh, Angela, we are going to have so much fun," she laughed.

Now that we had agreed on the terms, I did not want to waste another minute. I started firing questions, one after another. "Okay, Rose, how do I fix my life? Make some money to pay my debts? What do I have to do? Tell me! I'm ready!" I pleaded anxiously but sincerely.

"My dear, it is not really a question of doing. The correct question is the question of your lifetime and the question of the ages . . . It's the one that few people even think to ask themselves." At this she became contemplative.

"Okay," I said, now anxious to hear it. "What is the question? Come on, Rose. Tell me!"

"The question you must discover the answer to is: Who am I?

"Angela, when we become adults, grow up, leave the nest, so to speak, we think it works like this: first we *do*, then we *have*, and then we *be*. We do something to make a living, and we think that when we have enough of whatever it is we are seeking . . . money, fame, security, nice homes and fancy cars . . . then we will be happy. Most people tie up their feelings about themselves with what other people think of them or what they possess. Whenever you get your self-worth from anyone or anything other than from inside, you are sure to be unhappy. In fact, I think the outside world must be programmed to let us down over and over just to help us learn that lesson.

"If you strive for things on the outside and forget about who you are on the inside, you will find yourself compromising who you are for what you want. Ironically, what we think will make us happy all through our lives is way off the mark.

"By discovering the truth of who you are and deciding to live according to that truth, you will become an authentic human being. After all, we are first and foremost human *beings*. Not human *doings*." With that she giggled as if she had made the most delightful joke. However, only she was laughing. Me? I was just confused.

Seeing this, Rose gently reached for my journal, and taking out her pen, she wrote on the first blank page: "Who am I?"

"Rose, I would say I am Angela, daughter of Joan and Sam Edwards. I'm pretty sure that is not the kind of answer you are looking for. Can you give me a little more direction?"

"Angela, I can tell you that the answer is deep inside you at the very core of your being. Spend some time in quiet contemplation. You can pray about it or sit peacefully and listen. This is not an easy question to answer, so be gentle with yourself. When you get a thought, you can write it down. It might take you a few days to figure it out. You can spend time thinking about the lessons you learned in your dream. All these will help lead you to your answer."

Before I even thought about it, the question erupted from inside me like a volcano without warning. "Did you make me have that dream?"

"Oh, my heavens, child, *no*. Absolutely not. That was all your doing." Rose sat there for a few minutes, both stunned and amused by my question. After she recovered from the shock, she shook her head back and forth, adding, "My goodness, what will you come up with next?"

There was a moment of silence, and then I changed the subject. "Rose, at first I thought you were just a little, old lady with a bag full of memories, old stories, and little sayings you'd saved that caught your eye. They were nice stories, but I just couldn't see what they could mean to me personally. Now I look back and see that they were all geared to getting my attention about the deeper meaning of life."

Rose just looked at me, a sweet, little smile on her face.

"Rose, I want to apologize to you. I thought your mind was getting feeble. To me, you didn't look like you were using common sense sitting out here with your belongings loosely at your side. What is the deal with that? Why don't you have any worry for yourself?"

"Angela, I'll give you a short answer today . . . but later we will talk about it more. Remember, I told you that my life fell apart many years ago? I thought I was doomed. But then, suddenly, good things started happening to me. No matter how terrible the circumstance, everything would turn out just fine. I recognized that I was truly being taken care of. At first, I was totally mystified by it. But then I decided that I was like the birds and the lilies."

"Huh? Birds and lilies?"

Rose laughed out loud. "I guess that does sound funny, huh?" She laughed again. "Yes, you know . . . from the Bible. Remember how it says something like, see the lilies of the field; they toil not, and yet I care for them? And the birds do not sow or reap?"

We both laughed now, myself reassured once again that Rose had all her wits about her, and Rose tickled that I must have wondered about her sanity again for a moment. When our laughter died down, I took a moment to think about the lilies and birds. Something wasn't sitting quite right with that whole idea.

"But Rose, I've grown up with a strong work ethic. Please forgive me, but you're old, so you don't have to work anymore, but I sure don't think it is God's idea for all of us to just be deadbeats."

Rose laughed again. Obviously, she found the subject quite funny. "Angela, you are so much fun now that you have an open mind. I know this bird and lily subject has you really puzzled. I'll tell you what. I want to let you stew on that one a little. If you think about it some more, I'm sure you will see what I'm talking about."

Then Rose laughed again. She was obviously tickled with her newfound friend. "I'll give you two hints." Pretending to be insulted by my earlier comment, she said, "First, the birds and the lilies are not deadbeats!" Then she paused for a moment, as if she were thinking of something cryptic. "And second, there are two *be's* involved in the answer." Rose laughed uproariously.

"Bees?" I wrinkled up my face in confusion. "Rose, I already know about the birds and the bees."

That started Rose on another fit of laughter that was so contagious I joined her. We stopped momentarily, looked at each other, and broke down again. Rose pulled her hanky out from under her watchband, dabbed the tears from the corners of her eyes, and exclaimed, "Oh, Angela, you are just too much!"

With that, she reached into her bag and pulled out a blank index card and a bright red pen with ribbon and bells dancing on the top of it. Hiding the card from my view, she wrote on it and then turned it upside down as we said good-bye for the day.

"Angela, I have to run along now. But tonight your card will be a fill-in-the-blank. Do spend some extra time thinking

about who you really are, won't you? Write it in your journal, and we'll talk about it tomorrow."

A huge smile splashed across her face as Rose handed
me the card and reached down for her bag. In a moment,
she was off, clomping happily down the sidewalk in her
high heels.

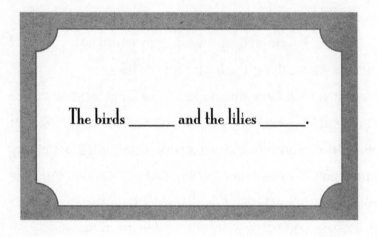

The birds _____ and the lilies _____.

# Chapter 20

All the way home, I was contemplating birds and lilies, deciding to ignore the part about the bees. Heaven only knows that I was not planning to discuss my sex life with the baglady.

Looking back on it now, it should come as no surprise to me that all varieties of lilies were blooming in the planted areas on my walk home. The garden center had daylilies, in sunshine yellow, and the fancy double orange ones, too. Street florists had huge vases of water with fresh-cut pink and white tiger lilies wrapped up ready for commuters to take home. As I made a quick stop at Wal-Mart, I found they were already stocking Easter lilies, and the scent met me as I walked in the door. They hadn't been there yesterday, had they?

My goodness, they were beautiful, and their fragrance was out of this world. There were some miniature ones in three-inch pots. The blossom was almost as big as the pot. I couldn't resist. A loaf of bread, milk, and a couple of Lean Cuisine made it into my basket along with a little lily for the kitchen table. My flower got all kinds of attention from people I passed on the way home. Several exclaimed that it was the first one they'd seen this year. Funny, they were walking the same streets as I was. Lilies were everywhere that day. *How had they missed them? It must have been the amazing scent of that little Easter lily that caught their attention.*

Spring was truly sprung, as the saying goes. Robins with their bright orange breasts were busy building nests to cradle the sky-blue eggs of their soon-to-arrive baby birds. Sparrows and wrens were working in frenetic preparation, as well.

The baglady was right about one thing: the birds, at least, were not deadbeats. But they didn't have jobs, not the way I see jobs, anyway. They were just busy being birds.

Arriving home, I was starved and popped a Lean Cuisine

into the microwave, grabbed the salad fixings out of the refrigerator, and took a swig out of a new bottle of spring water. I finished putting up the groceries and sat the journal on the table. In five minutes, I was eating dinner with my lily right in front of me, blooming its little heart out and casting a lovely scent throughout the loft.

Taking my commitment to the baglady seriously meant I was duty bound to complete the homework. Opening my journal, the index card was tucked into the same page as the question, "Who am I?" I decided the fill-in-the-blank card would be the best place to start.

Skipping a few pages in the journal to allow for an answer to the question Rose had written, I decided to go back to the Bible verse. I was surprised I could find my old Bible, because I certainly hadn't been reading it lately. There was something comforting about opening the leather-bound book. I found the passage and then wrote it in my journal: *Consider the lilies of the field, how they grow: they neither toil nor spin, yet I tell you, even Solomon in all his glory was not arrayed like one of these.* And then I searched and found the other passage I was looking for: *Look at the birds of the air: they neither sow nor reap nor gather into barns, and yet your heavenly father feeds them.*

Then I sat and pondered the whole thing. *What was God trying to tell us? I know it isn't to sit on our butts and do nothing . . . So what does it all mean? What does the baglady think it has to do with my life? I'll just concentrate on seeing what is so special about the birds and bees. No, I mean the birds and lilies.*

Just in my short walk from the store to home earlier, I had encountered so many people who commented on my one little lily. The fragrance caused them to turn and then see it in my arms. There were smiles and happy little conversations. And, of itself, the lily was really doing nothing. It was just . . . being a lily, and from that people were breathing in its scent, smiling, and talking to each other. The tiny lily was such a simple thing, and yet it had the power to affect the state of mind of the people through whose lives it briefly passed. Thinking about the little white blossom and all that had occurred on the way home, I was taken aback by the attention that was raised by the sight and smell of my little flower. That was kind of amazing.

I'd already noticed that the birds kept busy. Unlike people who can consciously decide what they will do, the birds just naturally fulfill their place in the world. *They do*

their bird thing, whatever that is. *Make nests, lay eggs, fly . . .
and some of them eat the mayflies*, I thought, remembering
the poem that Rose had given me a while back.

I picked up the card again, rolled it around in my fingers, and tapped it on the table while trying to put it all
together. *What have I experienced today, and what had the
baglady said earlier?* I recalled her saying that we humans
have it all backward. Rose said that before the idea of doing
things and having things came into play, we were first and
foremost meant to be human *beings*. I gave special emphasis in my mind to the word "beings," because Rose had
made such a production of it when she spoke to me.

*Oh, my gosh! I've got it!* I grabbed a pencil from the
counter and filled in the blanks.

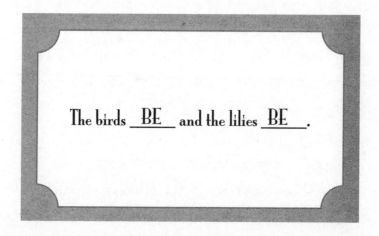

The birds __BE__ and the lilies __BE__ .

*Rose, Rose, Rose,* I thought. *You are such a character. It's two be's, just like you said.* I figured that wherever she was that night as the sun went down and the moon and stars filled the sky, she was probably having a good laugh on me.

# Chapter 21

T he evening had turned out kind of chilly, and I was trying to keep from firing up the heater again, so I boiled some water for hot tea and prepared to dig in for a long session of introspection. I threw a big, fluffy blanket on the overstuffed couch and pulled a little side table within reach, supplied with all the evening's possible needs: my journal, a box of chocolate-chip cookies, a pencil, and an oversized mug of tea. Crawling into my fuzzy cocoon, I figured it was going to be a long but productive night.

I had to at least make a stab at the question Rose had written down, but I had no idea where to begin. My total identity had gone down the toilet with my career and my marriage. Frankly, I had no idea who I was, at least from the standpoint the baglady was looking for.

For a long time, I sat there mindlessly sipping my tea. No thoughts entered my head. I was staring a hole through the opposite wall of the room and out into the darkness. I didn't even want to pull myself back. Without the things that gave me marketable value, I was nothing. I don't know how long I sat there, but in the quiet, I occasionally, for fleeting moments, would catch a hazy, distant hint of something . . . And then, as quickly as it came, it would escape me before I could actually force it into my conscious mind. It was like when you wake up from a dream; you want to recall it, but can't quite make it out.

What kind of answer was the baglady looking for? If I should be a human being first, before anything else, what would that look like? The birds and lilies have got it made. They just do what comes naturally to them. But, who am I?

I began to scan my recent memories to recall the different things Rose had given me and we had talked about. Then I thought back to the day when I practiced seeing everything as God's. Of everything she had shared with me, the lesson of that experience was the most profound. I thought back to the story of the rabbi's gift, where the monks started treating each other and themselves in a new way. And then my mind jumped to the greatest commandment: Love the Lord God with all your heart and your neighbor as yourself. I guess if I had to pick one sentence to sum up what the Bible was trying to teach us, it would be that one. And if everything is God's, then that includes me. I saw that it was true, but I didn't actually feel it, if you know what I mean.

I looked down at Rose's handwriting on the page: "Who am I?" I decided to write, "I am a child of God." As soon as I started writing, the words to a Sunday school song from my childhood came to me, and I started to sing it. Feeling kind of silly, I sang very quietly under my breath, just to get the words out. "Jesus loves the little children, all the children of the world. Red and yellow, black and white, they are precious in his sight. Jesus loves the little children of the world." I knew he loved me when I was little. I was then, and always will be, a child of God.

I hadn't thought of God like that in a long, long time. It's been a battle, instead, feeling guilty, angry, tortured, and unloved. Years of crying out in pain had left me thinking I was never heard or answered.

Then I thought back to how Rose had recounted my life back to me soon after we met. How she had shown me that God had been there all along. He was answering me according to my most predominant thoughts, giving me what I unknowingly was praying for . . . year after year after year. Quietly in the background, while I yelled at him every night, he was loving me every minute.

Suddenly, I felt it. And at that moment, I was overcome with love for him. Tears of gratitude overflowed from my eyes. My heart was finally open to welcome the one who had loved me always and would always be there for me. *He loves me! He really, really loves me! He never gave up on me!*

I flipped off the light and sat in my blanket cocoon, bathed in the warmth of a love I had never felt before. I didn't want anything to steal my attention, to take away this wonderful feeling. I had never felt so blessed or so happy in my entire life. As long as I sat there, I was in heaven, totally blissful, in need of nothing but him. I'm sure I was still smiling when I fell into a serene sleep, finally accepting the truth of who I am.

I am a beloved child of God.

# Chapter 22

When I woke up the next morning, the glow of the previous night's realization was still with me. I lay there for a few minutes basking in the overwhelming safety I was feeling.

Getting up, I walked toward the kitchen. Mmm . . . the exquisite fragrance of the Easter lily wafted through the loft. As I sat with my coffee, I noticed the stack of index cards Rose had given me. I picked them up and started to leaf through them, reflecting on each one. There was one I just couldn't get past. It was about my thoughts being powerful enough to change the world. I just couldn't grasp that one. I slipped it in my pocket, wanting to ask Rose about it.

Walking toward the park later that morning, I wondered how it could possibly be that one person's thoughts could have that much impact on the world. As I sat down next to the baglady, I handed her the card in question.

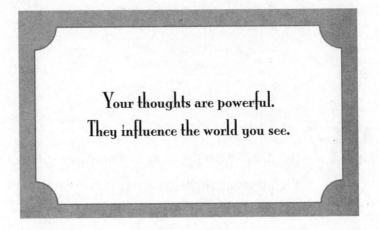

Your thoughts are powerful.
They influence the world you see.

She glanced at the card and handed it back to me. "Yes, I gave this to you quite a while ago. And as I recall, it didn't make much of an impression then. Would you like to talk more about it now?"

She smiled ear to ear as she looked over at me, nodding in the affirmative.

"Well, my dear," she giggled, "let's talk about gardening, shall we? The words on that card are as scientific as planting a garden."

"Okay?" I stammered, reluctantly playing along with her little tangent.

"A perfect conversation for spring." She paused for a moment, clearly enjoying the confused look on my face as she shot me an impish grin. "Okay, let's say you go to the garden center and get a package of petunia seeds. You plant them, and soon, up pop little petunia plants. You aren't disappointed. When they start to bloom, you're thrilled. You planted petunias, and that's what came up.

"Thoughts are just like petunias. Not very many people realize that they are planting 'thought' seeds all the time. Thought seeds are very hardy, very powerful. They will grow anytime." She laughed. "Plant a petunia seed; you get petunias. Plant seeds of love or kindness, and you'll reap a joyful harvest. Plant seeds of hatred, and you should not be surprised if your life is full of weeds and thistles."

Then she paused again as her demeanor became serious. "Angela, I just get tired of using the exact verses sometimes. I figured that a more thought-provoking statement might work for its shock value. You know, people have heard those Bible verses so many times; they have memorized them and quoted them forever. And yet, how many really look deeply at their underlying meaning? How many claim the truth for themselves and incorporate it into their lives? Live as if it is true? What I am asking here is, how many really take it to heart?

"I'll give you some Bible verses." She was acting kind of feisty, but at the same time I could tell she was using her attitude to accentuate a point. "Are you ready?" she asked, taking a deep breath as if she was going to have to project her voice to a multitude.

I just sat there, waiting for the next great flood.

Then with all the fervor of a spirit-filled evangelist, she let it rip. "You reap what you sow! Knock and the door will be opened! Ask and it will be answered! Seek and ye shall find!" Then her voice softened. "But the question is, do people really believe it? I mean, *really* believe it?"

Stepping down from her make-believe podium, she exclaimed, "*Whew!* Honey, don't get me started!" She laughed while fanning herself with her hand as if to cool herself down.

I blinked my eyes and sat there stunned. *Where did all that come from?* I thought. Right before my eyes she had taken on the attitude of an old-fashioned preacher.

With a slightly gentler demeanor, she continued, "The problem is that people have a preconceived idea about the way God answers prayer, and that preconceived idea is dead wrong a lot of times.

"Everybody knows the story of the man who refused help in a horrific flood that was engulfing his whole area. When the floodwaters were at the end of his street and all the other neighbors were leaving their homes, they offered to help him get himself and a few of his precious things out. He refused. Later, as the waters rose above his foundation and a foot up into his home, some people in a rowboat came by and offered to take him to safety. Then, as he was on his roof, his entire house filled with the floodwaters, the National Guard helicopter begged him to let them fly him to safety. Each time, his answer was, 'God will save me.'

"The old man ended up drowning, and when he was sitting in heaven at the feet of God, he complained, 'I had so much faith in you. I never doubted it, no matter what happened, and when I really needed you, you didn't save me.'

"God just shook his head. He had heard different versions of the old man's story throughout eternity. Then he said, 'I sent your neighbors, I sent the rowboat, and I sent the helicopter. You refused them all.'

"I think one of the biggest problems we have is not that God is not saving us; it is that we expect it to be on *our* terms. We often can't see the truth when it is staring us right in the face."

She was thoughtful for a moment and then continued, "Let's take, for example, a business owner and career woman. She knocks at God's door and says, 'I hate my life. I want out of this.' Since God doesn't communicate with a big, booming, God-type voice blasting down from the heavens, he sent her several opportunities that would move her in that direction. One, in particular, should have been pretty obvious. It looked like a big, powerful New York businessman who wanted to expand his product offerings. Their lines would have worked together perfectly. He had a huge company, and he wanted to buy hers. They had several days of serious conversation with his board of directors all around the table in his posh New York showroom.

"The offer was a good one. She would have become an instant millionaire in the deal. She knew that and was excited. He was planning a trip to visit her factory as the final step in the agreement, and she abruptly called the whole thing off. Why? The answer to her prayer did not look like what she expected. This wealthy businessman was going to take all the manufacturing to India. And she couldn't get past the idea that her employees were going to lose their jobs."

Finishing her story, the baglady looked at me, smiled, and gently patted my hand. "Does anything about that story ring a bell for you, dear?"

She had just repeated back a piece of my past that she had absolutely no way of knowing. I was dumbfounded. That was exactly what had happened two years ago in my very own life. While I sat there dazed, she changed the subject and started over as if we had just said hello.

"How are you this beautiful morning, Angela?"

At that point, shocked at the latest mystery of the baglady, I didn't know what to say. So, operating on autopilot, I dutifully answered her greeting. "Ah . . . I'm doing well," I said, still a bit dazed. Then I added happily, "I figured out who I am!"

"That is wonderful, dear. And I can't wait to hear all about that. But first, how about writing a little more in your journal? Then we can discuss all of your entries at the same time.

"I want you to remember back a few weeks ago, before we met. Think back to your state of mind. Write at least two pages of some of the thoughts and feelings you were having back then, the days before we met."

With that, Rose turned and took my hands in hers and cautioned me. "My dear, this exercise could be very painful. But it will be so helpful to you.

"You know, several times during our friendship, I have reminded you that everyone, no matter what it may look like, is always doing the best they can." Then she squeezed my hands for emphasis and looked into my eyes with earnest. "Remember, that applies to you, too. And as you write down that old self-talk, please don't feel guilty. Just put your pencil to the page and write it all down. Don't judge it. That is not the purpose here.

"After that, I want you to write down what your thoughts and feelings have been like over the past forty-eight hours. This one will probably be a lot more fun, but be sure to do both assignments to the best of your recall. And complete it as quickly as you can. Do not take time to analyze it. Just write," she reiterated, "at least two pages for each.

"I am going to take a stroll through the park to give you enough time for your assignment. I'll get us a little treat while I'm gone, and we'll have a wonderful discussion about everything when I get back."

With that, she pulled out her little jingle-bells pen and opened my journal to a blank page. She held up the pen, as if she were going to drop the starting flag at the racetrack.

"On your mark, get set, *go!*" She thrust the pen into my hand and left me alone on the bench to recount my past.

Rose came back with two cups of hot cocoa and some warm Krispy Kreme donuts just as I was finishing my final thoughts. It had been a cool morning, so the warm snack was perfect.

As we sat side by side enjoying our morning break, I asked, "Rose, do you wonder how you and I ever met in the first place? I mean, we are a pretty unlikely match, don't you think?"

She flashed a huge smile in my direction. "It was a delightful little miracle, wasn't it? I don't know when I've had so much fun. It's not every day that an older lady such as myself has the pleasure of the company of a bright, young woman of your character." She grinned.

Once we had finished our treat and wiped the sugar off our fingers, Rose continued, "So, what can you tell me about your writing?"

I plunged in. "Well, I'm painfully aware of what a bitter person I had become. I'm especially ashamed at how many evil thoughts I had toward others. Rose, almost no one was exempt. I envied everyone who had money, a career, or a family. As it turns out, back when I still owned my business and was yelling at God to get me out, I rationalized that my caring and concern for my employees and products seemed to balance things out. But since then, with all my other problems, I had become one wretched person. I'll tell you what. If I'd been you, and I ran into me, I would have turned tail and never looked back."

Rose smiled softly and waited for me to continue.

"And Rose, you were right. I was getting exactly the kind of life that I was spending my time thinking about. It was getting worse by the day.

"Then I met you. And when my car broke down, and I couldn't run away, I hid from you. Even then, you never wavered in your resolve. It's kind of a sweet, little story when I think about it, the way you put up with me. Somehow my venomous attitude didn't faze you in the least, no matter what I did."

Returning to the assignment, I continued. "And then I wrote pages and pages about all the things I have been thinking and feeling in the last couple of days, the questions I was asking in my mind and questions I was asking out loud. I was wondering about the answers and noticing what was happening around me. When I started wanting to understand you and the ideas you are sharing, well . . . it is like a miracle.

"For the past few days, so many coincidences have been happening. With me changing my attitude from sarcastic to sincere, answers are coming and my needs are being met. Remember how I found that $100 in my shoe, enough to get me through two weeks? And then you told me that you could teach me things that would help me within that amount of time. It's just uncanny how much things have changed in only a few short days.

"You'll never believe what happened this morning. The tow-truck driver called me to ask if he could drop by to talk with me about my car. I had been so preoccupied that I had completely forgotten about it being on his lot.

"Well, I started to tell him that I couldn't swing the repairs yet, but he stopped me, saying that we could talk about it when he got to my place. Rose, when he got to my house he was driving my car, and it was running perfectly. And it was all shined up like new. Inside and out!

"The driver told me he felt really bad for me and could tell I was having a hard time of it. He said he just happened to have the refurbished part my car needed and installed it for me. Can you believe that, Rose?

"He said he had some extra help on the lot one day, and so he had them detail it. I feel like I've got a brand-new car. It looks so wonderful. He said that he had received that payment from my insurance company for the towing fee yesterday and that I could just consider the rest a gift. Isn't that amazing?

"And, Rose, people have been so much nicer to me, in general—like holding doors open for me. Just simple things like that. I must tell you, I'm really blown away by what has happened. It's given me hope."

She was tickled pink with my report. I could see that by the huge smile on her face. "Angela, in the past we have talked about several things that all play into the discussion I want to have with you today. They intersect like the fingers as they come together to complete your hand. When we first met today, you brought up the card that says: 'Your thoughts are powerful. They influence the world you see.' Then I compared it to some verses out of the Bible. Another card was: 'What you focus on expands.' Pay very close attention today, my dear. Because understanding what I am about to share with you, and then putting it into practice in your daily life, is so important to your happiness on earth.

"Let's talk about how these ideas all work together. You can see just from what you wrote this morning that you do not have a waking minute that is empty of a thought or feeling about something. We've all got chatter going on in our heads. It's nonstop. As we discussed before, those thoughts and feeling, combined with your actions, are your unceasing prayer.

"Not many people realize that the more they think about something, the bigger it is going to get in their life. Whether it is a positive or negative thought makes absolutely no difference. You will get more in your life of everything you think about. If you have any doubt about the truth of that statement, I would suggest that you continue to write an overview of your thoughts at the end of every day for several weeks. Then compare that with a separate page or two telling what is happening in your life on a day-by-day basis.

"If you spend a lot of time being grateful for the good things, counting your blessings, so to speak, you will have more good things come to you. If your time is spent worrying about money, your money woes will become bigger. Think more about anyone who aggravates you, and things will get worse between you.

"Do you understand what I am saying, Angela? It is your prayer, and it is constantly being answered. That is why it is so very important to learn to be mindful of your thoughts.

"You can see the same message in the Bible verses. Knock and the door will open. Knock at the door of joy with a heart full of love, and the door of happiness will open. Knock at the door of hatred, and that is what you will receive.

"Seek and ye shall find. Seek to see the goodness in the world, and you will find it. Seek to blame others and look for their failures, and you will see an ugly world. We are creatures with free choice. And you are constantly choosing with your thoughts and feelings."

There are no idle thoughts.

Then she reached into her bag and pulled out another card.

"Angela, earlier you gave me the card that said your thoughts are powerful and influence the world."

"Well, Rose, at first I really thought it was an arrogant statement to think that God makes everything work out especially for me. But now I think I understand what you are saying. It isn't just for me. It is true for everyone.

"The Bible verses support the same idea. Because each person has different thoughts and feelings, they are each getting to experience life from their own unique perspective. Our most predominant thoughts shape our life. Or, in other words, we all get to experience the world that we, ourselves, choose. The bad deal is that I would bet that most people are like me. I bet they don't have any idea that they are actually choosing their lives with their thoughts. I have been living my life as if I were a victim of the world that others made, and now I see that I have been the one calling the shots all along."

I sunk down lower on the bench, ashamed of the realization I had just stumbled onto. "Rose, I feel awful. I've thrown a lot of blame on other people. To say nothing of the wars I have waged against God. How can I ever be forgiven?"

She wrapped a fragile arm around me. "My dear, would you hold it against a child who burns herself on a stove?"

"I think this is a little more than a kid with a stove, Rose," I retorted, thinking she was making light of the sins of my lifetime.

"Angela," she shook my shoulders a little bit to accentuate her excitement, "you are feeling depressed, and I'm sitting here imagining that all heaven is rejoicing at your waking up. God isn't the mean, old tyrant waiting to pound you for your mistakes. Every minute of every day, he is rooting for you. He's giving you new opportunities, new chances to choose the loving answer. Every day of your life, until one day . . . well, never mind about that; that is a topic for another day. We have a big enough fish to fry today on this subject.

"Always remember, no matter what anyone, including you, has done . . ."

"I know. I know. Everyone is doing the best they can." I still felt depressed. No matter what celebration she thought was happening in heaven, I felt like scum.

Ignoring my nasty attitude, Rose just went right on with her lesson. "Angela, we should alter that statement a little bit. Everyone is doing the best they can based on what they know, and what they really and truly believe.

"The longer I live, the more I realize that most people feel inadequate. Many are plagued with feeling unworthy, not good enough. So without even thinking about it, in their self-talk, their thoughts and feelings, they put themselves down. They recount the ways in which they think they fall short. The more they judge themselves, the more they judge others. Without even realizing it, that negative attitude becomes their prayer.

"Just think back to yourself a few weeks ago. It's not just people on the lower rungs of the ladder that feel this way. It goes all the way up to the top of most organizations. The only way people will ever break out of the pattern that keeps them judging themselves and others is to step back from their incessant running, their back-breaking schedules, and get in touch with what is at the very root of their life here on earth.

"It is a monumental problem. And it all stems from one thing. People have forgotten who they really are, so they run scared through this life, putting each other down instead of lifting each other up, hating others for their weaknesses rather than seeing that it calls for compassion. There are millions of people on the earth, and yet so many feel lonely. That loneliness leads to unhappiness, and that unhappiness leads to a lifelong prayer that will bring more and more unhappiness until they learn to stop the dizzying merry-go-round and get off.

"A few, like you and me, are the lucky ones. It is not so easy to jump out of a life whirling out of control. In all their terrible fear and unhappiness, the fear of being beaten and bruised in the fall is even scarier. Most stay on, hanging on for dear life, afraid of jumping and fearing that their strength will fail and they will fall anyway. Even many highly successful people are terribly afraid of failure; afraid someone will come along who is better than them and push them out of their position. It is the merry-go-round from hell.

"But we know nothing else; we think that this must be the way it is supposed to be. After all, everyone else is on the same crummy ride.

"We judge the people with addictions, but we need to see clearly that we all have our addictions. We all cling to something that helps us make it through the days and nights of our lives of *doing*. All this happens before we ever even have time to experience our true essence, as human *beings*.

"So you see, Angela, everyone really is doing the best they can. And that does include you. Be grateful, Angela. You are forgiven. You and I are blessed in more ways than you even realize.

"For you see, we have been the lucky ones. Without the guts to jump off, somehow God blessed us and plucked us off the incessant, ever-spinning merry-go-round. For me, it was years ago, and for you, only recently. Oh, yes, at first I thought it was a fate worse than death, just as you did. But in time, help came to show me the way. And in your time . . . well, we found each other.

"Because of the most fortunate of unfortunate events, you and I are here on this bench, on a beautiful spring day, eating donuts, talking and laughing . . . and learning what it takes to find true happiness."

"You're right, Rose. A gorgeous day it is! And . . . I really am glad I met you. You know, we've talked all this time, and we haven't even discussed the homework assignment I did last night."

"Oh, my goodness, you're right. The time has just flown by," Rose replied as she glanced down at her watch. "Would you mind if we started out again tomorrow morning?"

I could tell that Rose was pleased with how far we had come that day, but I also noticed that she was looking a little tired, so I readily agreed. "That will be fine," I replied. "How about if I walk you home this afternoon?" I asked while picking up her bag.

"No, no, my dear. I have errands to run, and certainly you could use some time to yourself. You run along now and have a nice evening."

We both got up at the same time, and I kissed her on the cheek as I transferred her bag by slipping the handles onto her arm. We said our good-byes and both took off in opposite directions down the familiar street.

# Chapter 23

Walking home, I was kind of glad we kicked off a little early. Rose had given me a lot to think about. One thing I decided to do was to keep up with the journal every day. I decided to summarize all my thoughts daily and made a mental note to be sure to include all the downer thoughts as well as the positive ones. If I could stop judging myself, and just write down a true accounting, I knew I would get a clearer picture of my life.

I also vowed to take a few minutes every evening before going to bed to write down several things I am grateful for. Thinking back to the first night I did that assignment, I smiled at the memory of the moon shining in on me. Funny, there must have been hundreds of nights when it had done that, but I had never noticed it before.

Looking back at how much of life I had never noticed, I fell into a depressed state again. *My, how fast my emotions can seesaw up and down.* Just then, my journal slipped from my hand and made a loud smack as it hit the sidewalk. Leaning down to pick it up, I remembered that I would be better off concentrating on positive thoughts. *Feed the white wolf,* I thought to myself, and then I went back to thinking about what else I'd like to write about every day.

Since meeting Rose, I'd had several dreams that seemed to follow what I was learning, so I decided to put a tablet by my bed and write down everything I could remember about them when I woke up in the morning. No matter whether they made any sense or not, I'd just write it all down.

All these things would get me in the habit of staying in touch with what might be going on in my head. I made the conscious decision to become aware of my thoughts and feelings. It was a good walk home, and I felt empowered by my decisions.

Later in the evening, after writing the things I was grateful for, the book flipped open to the question written in

Rose's shaky cursive. And then I read my answer below: "I am a beloved child of God." I repeated it in my mind slowly, over and over as I turned out the light. Again, I slept peacefully until morning came with sunshine streaming in my window.

I opened the window wide and shouted out, "Good morning, world!"

Rushing to get ready, I was filled with anticipation about what the baglady would teach me that day.

The second I sat down beside Rose, I handed her my assignment: the birds and lilies card with the two *"be's"* inserted. Even though I had written my answer to "Who am I?" in the journal, I didn't show it to her. I decided to tell her instead.

She was still nodding with approval at the answers I showed her when I happily announced, "Rose, I am a beloved child of God!"

"Well . . . *that you are!*" Rose responded with a giggle. "What took you so long?" she chided, and then we both burst out laughing.

After our laughter had calmed down a little, she said with delight, "Oh, Angela, do you have any idea how much I love you?" And then she laughed some more through her tears. Soon her hanky was being pulled out of her watch-band and dabbed at the corners of her eyes again.

Even after her laughter stopped, she was still catching tears as they rolled down her cheeks. She wiped her eyes, saying, "Don't mind me. I'm just a silly, old fool. You'll see one day for yourself. As you get older, and your time on the earth gets shorter, everything becomes so much more precious. I cry every day, not for sadness, but for all the love I see in the world. One day, you'll see what I mean." She trailed off again, "You'll see."

I gave her a few minutes, let her have her cry. Soon she was back on track with me. "Angela, how about we start out with another writing exercise this morning?"

"Okay," I said, while handing over my journal to her again. She held it on her lap while explaining the assignment.

Her words were thoughtful as she spoke. "If a person truly knew themselves as a beloved child of God, came to earth straight from the loving arms of God the Father with all his blessing for a wonderful life, a life of their own choosing . . . then how would that child be in the world?"

As I opened my mouth to start to answer, she raised her finger to her lips to keep me from speaking.

"I want you to take a little time before you answer. Drink

in the magnitude of this question and of the answer that could set you free.

"The Holy Spirit's voice is very quiet. Until you make a concerted choice to be still and listen to that voice of peace, you will miss all kinds of opportunities to have an intimate communion with God.

"Angela, today is yours. Spend it in quiet contemplation. Walk in the park; take in the sights and the smells and the sounds of the earth. Let your heart lead today, and wherever it takes you, follow. If you feel you should write something down, write. And when that moment of inspiration is finished, follow again. Wander . . . if that is what you feel. Today, be totally at the whim of where your heart takes you. The rest of the day is yours."

Anxious at the thought of a day not filled with instruction from the baglady, I objected, "You mean you're not going to teach me today?" I pleaded, "But you promised to help me find answers, and a week goes very quickly. I hate to miss a day." I tried to convince her as my fear was rising quickly. "I'm scared, Rose." I pleaded with her as my lower lip began trembling.

With that, she hugged me to her frail, little body, and I felt an immediate comfort in her touch. She whispered to me, "My dear, there is something to learn from the silence. Something you cannot get by listening to an old lady jabber all day long. You'll be fine." As she pulled back and took my hands, she smiled confidently, looked into my eyes, and chirped, "Angela, you are going to have a wonderful day! It will be a lark. You'll see. Now run along. You've got the whole day. The world is your oyster."

After having grown so attached to her daily words of wisdom, I was still feeling jilted by this dear little grandmother figure, but she was so convincing that I agreed to go along with it. Once again, she motioned me to be on my way. I did leave, though feeling slightly dejected as I moved away from her and into the park.

# Chapter 24

Soon, I decided to stop and write down my assignment. As closely as I could remember, Rose had said, "If a person really knew that they were the beloved child of God, how would they be in the world?"

Jesus would be the perfect example, since he definitely knew he was God's beloved child. But then, it seemed preposterous and impossible to put me, or anyone else for that matter, in the same boat as Jesus. Dropping that train of thought, I got up and walked through the park.

The baglady's instructions had been to go with my gut—my words, not hers. I walked around aimlessly, more avoiding my assignment than trying to do it. It was around 11:30, and my stomach started growling. Being close to the loft, I went up and fixed myself a salad.

Several months earlier, a new restaurant had opened right next door. I'd been eating there far too often, and it was showing on my waistline. So I had vowed to myself that I would stay away from Logan's Grille. They had the best juicy, home-style hamburgers I had ever tasted, and all through my lunch, as I munched down on the salad, I couldn't stop thinking about those burgers. It aggravated me that I was still obsessing about it after rinsing off my dishes. Grabbing a bottle of water and running down the stairs, I knew I'd better get as far away as possible from Logan's before all resistance was lost.

An hour later, I had walked more than a mile away from the loft. I had taken my body away from the temptation, but my mind never left for one minute. The assignment had gotten no attention since I had passed by my favorite burger joint the first time. The butter-toasted bun, half a pound of lean ground beef topped with thick slices of onion and tomato, lettuce ruffled out around the bun. As I walked, in my mind I laid the top bun to the side, tipped up the mus-tard bottle, and drew long, lazy circles in sunshine yellow over the greens, replaced the top, and lifted it to my mouth. I was in hamburger heaven. I closed my eyes, right there on the street. *Mmmmmmmm.*

Still determined to resist, I walked fifteen additional paces farther away from my obsession. And then, as if I were on a drill team and had just been instructed to "about face," I turned around without any hesitation and ran the mile back to have my craving met. I alternated between beating myself up about my weak will and justifying my actions based on the fact that, once I got the hamburger, I would then at least be able to concentrate on my assignment.

Tom Logan, the owner, was sitting in the dining room when I arrived and asked me to join him. Once I sat down, I could see that he was distraught. So we started talking.

My meal arrived. I ate, and we talked about business strategies and what he could do to create better profits. When I was ready to leave, he thanked me for my suggestions and told me my lunch was on the house. It was the strangest thing, but just as I walked out the door, it occurred to me that I had not come for the hamburger at all. I felt certain that I had actually come because Tom needed someone to talk to that day. It made me feel so good to think that I was at the right place at the right time, and all under the guise of needing a hamburger. Knowing something powerful had just happened, I said a quick "Thank you, God" as the door closed behind me.

It was the most amazing feeling, to be used to help another person without my knowing it, or intending to do it. I felt goose bumps all over. This experience was just the push I needed to get me thinking about the question I was supposed to ponder. In all my life, I had never experienced anything that gave me more joy than the feeling I got as I left Tom's place. I was overcome with gratitude.

Stopping at the closest bench, I started writing.

If I knew without a doubt that I was the beloved child of God, I would trust him in all things. My prayer would be, Thy will, not mine, be done. Use me. Instead of trying to operate with my own agenda, I would follow him. I would be ever mindful of listening to the quiet place from which the Holy Spirit would show me the way.

I would never need to worry about anything, for I would know that he is watching over me just like the birds and the lilies. Not to be a deadbeat, not to be irresponsible, but only to be wholly available to live the

fullness of what I can be as a child of God on earth. I
would give up my ideas about what my life should be
and trust in his plan for me, to let him show me the
doors through which I most willingly would walk. To
send me where I am to go and to beckon me to silence
when he had something to tell me, and to hear him and
follow him in everything I do, with all my heart.

I had to laugh as I wrote the last sentence. It was an echo
of one of the cards Rose had given me. Without my consciously realizing it, all her wisdom had been sinking in.
*She'll be thrilled when I read it to her tomorrow. Where did
all those words come from?*

The late afternoon was getting a little chilly by the time
I finished writing, so I closed my journal and walked back
to the loft, well satisfied by my interactions with Tom at
the restaurant, as well as the wonderful lunch with which
he had gifted me. I was still so full that I skipped dinner,
took a quick shower, and decided to watch a little television
before turning in for the night.

The next morning, I was just walking down the stairs to
go meet Rose when there was a knock at the street-level

door. I hollered, "I'm coming!" and then raced down the stairs two at a time. Out of breath, I opened the door.

To my surprise, it was Tom. He said, "Angela, I had to come over to thank you for the time you spent with me yesterday. I was having a bad day, and you helped me more than you know." Then he paused for a moment and added, "And also to tell you . . . I know you were sent."

Well, if I had any doubts before that, Tom's acknowledgement was the icing on the cake. Once again, I was in awe of it, this power that could make all things work for good. I just thought I was craving a hamburger, but instead was allowing myself to be led.

# Chapter 25

I headed toward the park a lot earlier than usual, about a half-hour ahead of my normal schedule. As I rounded the corner and caught a glimpse of the baglady, I was so taken by the vision that I doubled back behind a bush before she saw me.

Our bench was at the very edge of a huge inner-city park, and it was not that unusual to see all kinds of small, wild animals, especially if you were to walk back into the forested area, but I had never seen anything but squirrels and birds when in the main park area. And yet, there was the baglady, sitting on the bench with a menagerie of all sorts of animals around her. A tiny chipmunk was perched on the seat within inches of her. There was a wren sitting on the armrest as she scattered breadcrumbs to a rainbow assortment of birds on the ground below. I spotted a doe just off to the side under the shade of a tree. As I stood there watching, a mother mallard with all her little ducklings in tow was cruising past on the sidewalk.

Rose was talking to them as if she knew each one. I was transfixed by the sight. The baglady looked like Mother Goose sitting there among the wild animals, turned gentle creatures in her presence. And then, as if to warn them that she would soon be meeting me, she raised her hands up joyfully and waved to them, as if cautioning them it was time to go back into the woods before the daily parade of human beings began in the park.

It struck me then, as never before, that she was so full of mysteries I may never understand. *Who is this little, old lady, teacher to me and friend to every creature of the park?*

After all the animals had left, she sat there in the same pose as she had every day, awaiting my arrival. *How often do the animals come to be fed by her? Why is she never afraid?* She was always confident, full of joy, and seemingly invulnerable to any potential harm. Rose was the embodiment of gentleness and unconditional love for everyone and every-thing in the world. She was in harmony with the whole of it. And I had been drawn to her.

Standing there in my hiding place, I considered asking her about her animal friends and then decided against it. Clearly, she was intending to keep that to herself. Other-wise, she wouldn't have sent them away before my arrival. At least for the time being, I decided not to mention it. If I was ever to understand the baglady, it was best if I followed the curriculum that she had laid out for me.

With that thought, I forced what I had just seen to the back burner and quietly relived what had happened to me yesterday. As soon as I had regained my focus, I walked out from behind the bush and back around the corner, waving as I saw her look in my direction.

Hugging her with excitement, I sat down and recounted what had happened with Tom. Then I opened the journal page to what I had written and handed it over to Rose.

She read it with great interest, and a broad smile flashed across her face as she finished. "You're coming right along, aren't you, Angela?" she commented, delighted with my answer. With that, she reached over and squeezed my hand.

"Your encounter with Tom certainly was timely. It is as if God was showing you an example of how blessed you could feel with him leading your life instead of you. Also, did you take note of the fact that your food was provided for you yesterday without your spending money for it? Tom didn't know that you were short on funds, and yet he fed you as a gift." Then she giggled and added, "It is such a lark to see how God handles things, isn't it?"

Then she continued, once again back in her instructor mode. "Many years ago, when I began to have similar experiences to the one you had yesterday, I started keeping notes in my journal about them. Over time, I could see that the occurrences were often directly related to the things I had been thinking and feeling. Time and again, answers came. It got to the point that I finally had to accept that it was more than coincidence. I could truly see that I was taken care of." Then she paused and added, "Just like the birds and lilies.

"After that," she continued, "I started to move toward whatever came to my attention each day. If people came to my mind, I would call them. If I felt a need to take a walk, I'd take a walk. Some days I would talk to people; other days I wouldn't speak to a soul. Occasionally, I would strongly feel that I had been sent, as you and Tom both realized had happened yesterday. Most of the time what I experienced was simply a feeling of peace and contentment. My life started to run smoothly. My needs were being met through means I never, in a million years, would have dreamed possible. My life became a miracle. And that is still the way I live today. Mostly, I'm just contented, but occasionally, when I meet someone like you . . . well, those are the very best days of all."

As she handed my journal back to me, she went on in a serious tone. "So, Angela, now that you have written what you would do if you believed 100 percent that you were a beloved child of God, how much of that are you willing to put into play in your daily life?"

I opened the book and looked again at what I wrote. "Well," I said, "even though I wrote this and believe that it is true, it is still kind of scary, you know? I've always taken such pride in standing on my own feet, guiding my own life. Rose, I've always seen strength in being able to make decisions for myself. To adopt that way of living would be entirely opposite of anything I've ever known. I have to admit that I wrote that answer in a state of euphoria, while I was high on the thrill of feeling like God was using me. I've never had that experience before and . . .

well . . . I just don't have the same confidence as you that it will always work.

"Like, for instance, I need to get a job, buy food, and try to get out of debt. I know this may sound silly because, after all, God is all-powerful and limitless . . . but it seems like he has so many more important things to do than guide my every step. I feel like I should be responsible for that. Otherwise, I'd be lazy. I just feel so responsible for my own life."

Rose nodded in complete understanding and said, "Angela, have you ever heard the Bible verse, the one that instructs us to become an empty vessel for God to fill? What do you think that means?"

"I think it means that we are supposed to free ourselves of our preconceived ideas and be open to following his lead. Look, I wrote something like that in my journal." With that, I opened the page and read to her.

> If I knew without a doubt that I was the beloved child of God, I would trust him in all things. My prayer would be, Thy will, not mine, be done. Use me. Instead of trying to operate with my own agenda, I would follow him.

"Rose, did you hear that? What I wrote was the same thing as that Bible verse but in different words."

Rose continued, "And back to your concern about working and eating . . . don't you suppose that if you stayed open to his leading that you would be shown the way? Don't you think that it is possible that in searching for a job, you would be led in a direction that would reveal it to you? Just look how persistent God was in getting you to go to Logan's Grille yesterday. Do you think he could lead you to your perfect vocation?"

"When you put it that way, I have to say yes. But I have to admit that I am torn. All my life I have been taught to stand on my own two feet and fight to overcome any obstacle that got in my way."

"You're right, Angela. Surrendering and giving someone else the chance to be in the driver's seat is a huge leap of faith. But, for me, it was only when I did turn it all over to God and gave up on all my preconceived notions that my life became truly blessed. Surrender is difficult and something we so often ignore. It is a truth discovered time and time again by the teachers we've been given," Rose declared with conviction.

"Life should be joyful, peaceful, and fulfilling. And yet we run, we work, we spread ourselves so thin that there is no time to enjoy just being alive." She softened, turned and took my hands in hers, and looked at me with such love and compassion in her eyes. Slowly, she whispered, "Angela, you have been running your own life for a long time, and it has not made you happy. Look at how many years you have been unhappy." Rose sat quietly, giving me time to think. Then she added, still in a whisper, "You can make a different choice and let God lead you instead, especially now that you know who you really are. As a beloved daughter of God, you can stand steadfast in that truth, and your life can be a reflection of knowing it. The choices you'll make and what you *do* will come from a different place. You have only to loosen your strong-as-steel grasp on what you have always thought was the way to be in this world, and instead, gently and tenderly hold hands with the truth.

"My dear, allowing God to lead you *is* the responsible approach. It is a path of such immeasurable fulfillment. You will be in awe when you see that you will always have everything you need. Your part is to continue to feed the white wolf. Live your life in gratitude, joy, peace, and forgiveness, and leave the details to God."

I was noticeably upset. I didn't know how a day that
started out so perfectly could be so unsettling only a few
hours later. It seemed like Rose was giving me a naive
answer to a serious problem. It just couldn't be that simple.

I had written that I would follow, and I wanted to
believe that it was possible to let go of all my worries and
trust . . . but the black wolf was growling at me so loudly
that I couldn't think straight. I made some excuse about
having to leave early. I needed time to think, to try to calm
myself down. It was clear to me that I couldn't concentrate
on feeding the white wolf while the black one was tearing
up my backside. Trying to mask my feelings of panic, I
made an excuse and got away from Rose and that bench as
quickly as possible. There were too many conflicting
voices in my head, and I needed desperately to calm the
inner turmoil before I exploded from all the emotions I
was feeling.

I walked calmly to the corner and a little past it so as not
to alarm Rose. Then I started to run. I ran like a crazy person. I ran as fast as I could, breathing so hard I thought my
heart would burst.

Finally stopping to catch my breath, I noticed that the
chaos in my brain had quieted, at least for the moment. I

was at a crossroads. I couldn't go back. My past life was gone. My judgments of what life should be like were pulling me in one direction. Respectable people pulled themselves up by their own bootstraps, did whatever it took to succeed. Happiness and inner peace were way down the list of priorities.

Then there was the baglady, encouraging me to see that life could be entirely different. She was the most peaceful and joy-filled person I had ever met; showing me the effects of gratitude, helping me to understand the personal nature of God's love, and guiding me on where to put my focus, how to direct my mind and heart.

The problem, as I saw it, was that in order to live the life she was showing me, I would have to take a giant leap of faith. I truly would have to turn my back on my old ways. The old ways were safe. And yes, they made for a miserable existence. They had never brought me the happiness I'd seen over the last week. As broke as I was, alone, in debt . . . even with all these problems, I had seen a glimpse of another way of looking at the world. I wanted that!

I thought for a few minutes more, mulling over both sides back and forth in my head like a Ping-Pong game. Then, suddenly, it occurred to me. I was going to have to kill off that black wolf before it dragged me back over the line to return to a life I no longer wanted. *I bet the baglady would know how to get the job done.*

With that thought, I turned around and, retracing my steps, ran back to our bench, hoping she would still be there.

# Chapter 26

"Angela!" There was a look of surprise on Rose's face. "You're back so soon?"

"I just needed a little time to sift through my feelings," I explained. "Rose, I see the way you are. You're always happy. You make everything look so easy, but you scared me this morning. I felt like I had to make a choice, and yet I'm not sure how it will all turn out."

Then she patted my spot on the bench as she said, "I was a little concerned about you when you left so abruptly."

"I realized that I'd have to make a choice. You know, run my own life or put myself in God's hands. From what you tell me, you were able to make that decision, and from everything I can see, it really has worked out for you. How did you do it?"

"Well, my dear, there is a very simple answer, but getting there does take a bit of a shift in your thinking. For me, I live by the guidance of my inner voice, the Holy Spirit, if you will. It is not a voice like you and I are using here to talk. It is more like a gentle nudging or a thought that comes to mind. It requires that you silence all the other conflicting voices in your head in order to hear the voice of God." The longer the baglady spoke, the more serious and contemplative she became. I could tell that she was trying to figure out how to help me truly grasp this very deep concept.

She continued, "For many people, it is hard to hear it. Actually, no, it is not hard to hear, but it is so easy to dismiss. It may seem frivolous and lacking importance, especially if you have a lot of contradictory thoughts going on in your head. Like, for instance, right now, you have lots of thoughts about finding a way to make money and pay bills. Then mixed in with that are your thoughts about your personal and career failures. Add to that those thoughts of hate directed toward the people in your life who have done you wrong. All those other things are much more urgent and carry a lot of negative emotion with them. All that inner turmoil can certainly drown out the very gentle voice of God."

She paused for a moment, deep in thought. Suddenly, her spirits seemed to brighten. She had come up with a solution to the dilemma of how to make me understand. With renewed enthusiasm for the teaching, she fished in the bag for her crazy jingle-bells pen.

"Okay, Angela, I've got an idea that will help you sift through some of that chaos in your mind." She shook the pen playfully, sending the sound of tiny tinkling bells like fairy dust around us. "With this, you can take those thoughts out of your mind and put 'em on paper, so you can see them more clearly."

She opened my journal and wrote the new assignment. She then showed me the page that said, "Write a list of the ways in which you believe that you have failed or fallen short and the reasons you are not worthy of a life of joy."

I sat there stunned. The baglady was always so upbeat, trying to pull me up out of the pit of despair, and now, with this assignment, it was like she was throwing me back into it headfirst.

"Rose?" I gasped, looking at her questioningly.

She just patted my hand and reassured me. "I know this one is going to be painful, so I'll sit here with you while you do it. Take your time. Write everything you can think of." She paused and then added with determination, "Don't worry, my dear, just write."

She sat. I wrote. And, yes, it was painful. Putting those thoughts on paper made me feel like I was convicting myself in some kind of legal proceeding. The baglady paid no attention to what I wrote; she just sat there holding the space.

Regardless of my misgivings, I recounted all the dismal failures of my lifetime. Once I got started, it wasn't difficult to get in touch with my self-hate, the many ways in which I didn't measure up. I filled both the left and right hand sides of the journal pages and then turned to start in on the next page. To my surprise, there was another assignment at the top of that page. Seeing that, I again flashed a questioning look in her direction.

Rose patted my hand, smiled, and remarked, "My dear, two full pages are enough for now. Certainly you have already listed the things that are most pressing and consuming your energy."

The next page's assignment said, "List the ways you have been let down or harmed by others."

I liked that one a lot better. Even though I recognized how easy it was to put myself down, I found it a lot easier to blame others for part of the downfall of my life. Misery loves company, as the old saying goes, and I definitely wanted to share the blame, if not find reasons why others had more responsibility for my downfall than I did. I excitedly wrote about their shortcomings, believing that if I could have wiped these people and circumstances out of my life, I would have been much happier. I filled the first two pages with ease, flipped the page, and continued. When I finished, I made a motion to hand Rose my confession. She only closed it and sat it back on my lap.

"Angela, in writing that, did you recognize and recall how often those thoughts actually go through your mind in a day?"

I nodded, again depressed by all my negativity. "Rose," I said slowly, "during our time together, I have tried really hard to learn from you. I want my life to be happy. I really do. Until this assignment, I thought I was doing pretty well. But the truth is, these things are crossing my mind on an ongoing basis."

"Angela, that exercise may have seemed like a step backward to you, but there is a very important lesson in it. When you are deeply hurt about something, you try to move forward by suppressing it. Then those bad feelings go underground, so to speak, where they smolder deep inside and eat at you. Even though you try to overcome them, they are still a smoldering fire just waiting for the next similar incident to occur. When that happens, it is like suddenly adding oxygen to the smoldering embers. All at once, those feelings are a raging blaze again. It's as if the most recent incident is simply adding another log to the fire.

"What we are doing with this exercise is to bring it all up to the surface." She continued to be very serious as she spoke.

Then, pausing again, she completely changed her tone to lightheartedness as she added with delight, "Today, my dear, you will become a firefighter." The baglady broke out in contagious giggles.

I smiled at her through my confusion. It seemed like I was on another roller-coaster ride of emotions today. She was dragging me up and down and up again. From past experience with her, I knew eventually she would make her point, so I concentrated on hanging on for the ride.

She was fishing for something in her bag again and presented me proudly with another card.

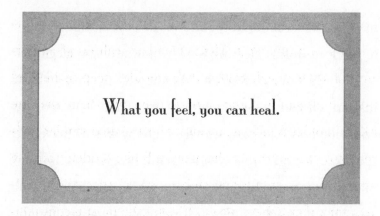

What you feel, you can heal.

I looked at it for a moment and then looked at her, perplexed. "Rose, first you tell me I'm going to be a firefighter, and then you give me this card. Forgive me, but I just don't see the connection."

She laughed again. "You'll see. My dear, you just brought many of your smoldering embers to your attention. Now you need to develop the skills to put out the fire. I must caution you, glossing over your hurts will not put out the fire. You have to consciously bring them to the surface and then change your mind. Today, and tonight for your assignment, you will deal with those things that you were able to think of today. But this skill of firefighter will be one that you will have to use over and over, anytime you notice that you are holding negative feelings against yourself or others. This is so important, because holding grudges or judgments will mask the voice of the Holy Spirit inside of you. And you want to be clear. In that clearing is a life of beauty and elegance.

"I could talk forever on this subject . . . but I think, instead, I'll give you some homework. Then, by tomorrow, you will be well on your way through my special firefighter training. Tonight you will have an experience that will make today's ups and downs all worth it, Angela. Your assignment tonight is to transform those negative thoughts and experiences into blessings."

Rose was so excited as she began to tell me about "The Blessing Lady," as if she were a tooth fairy of sorts for grown-ups.

"Angela, back when I was experiencing similar fears, doubts, and betrayals as the ones you are holding in your heart now, I had a friend who I continued to go to with all my belly aching and bad attitudes. I hate to admit it now, but I was really attached to my judgments. I was hard on other people and even harder on myself.

"She would patiently listen to me tell my sad stories. When I was finished, she would console me for a while. But then, before our visit was over, she would always turn the table on the situation and encourage me to find the blessing in whatever had happened. At first, I was annoyed and wanted to hold on to my complaints and judgments, so it was difficult for me. But she would work with me until we could see that I had benefited in some way from each difficulty. It was always so fascinating to see the blessing."

Suddenly, the baglady seemed to be filled with childlike innocence as she chattered on with overflowing joy at being able to share this with me. She was almost giddy, as if she were experiencing it all over again.

"Angela, in the end, I could see it. There really, truly always was a blessing to be found! And that helped me see that I really am being taken care of, even when things seem to go wrong. When I looked deeply, I could always see the blessing."

She was still as excited as could be as she sent me home with the assignment. I was to find the blessings in all the bad feelings I held against myself and others on my list.

"Angela," she said as I was leaving, "forgiveness is the water that will put out all your fires of blame and guilt. And once you can find the blessing, you will realize that there is nothing to forgive. It will change your life forever!"

# Chapter 27

The next morning, as I approached our bench, Rose had her head buried inside her bag. All sorts of papers and assorted objects were scattered around at her feet and covering the bench. Thinking that whatever she was doing might give me a clue into the mysteries of that bag, I once again stepped back a couple of steps and decided to just watch her for a few minutes.

She was intent on her work, organizing pages and cards into two different stacks, looking each one over before she placed it on the pile of her choice. She had her jingle-bells pen out, and occasionally she would stop and make a few notes in a separate notebook. I watched as she unwrapped a peppermint and popped it in her mouth. There was a little bag of cookies by her side. There seemed to be nothing unusual about her activities as she sat there, so I moved toward my baglady.

Engrossed in her organizing, she didn't even look up as I approached. Concerned about startling her, I called her name before getting too close. "Rose, good morning," I said in a singsong voice.

She looked up and smiled. "Oh, my dear, I'm afraid you have caught me in a mess. Here, let me clean off your spot." As she was cleaning off the bench, I looked around to see if there were any unusual animals in the area. Nothing seemed the least bit magical about her today. *Interesting.*

Then she patted my spot as she asked me, "How are you this morning? I was a little concerned about you yesterday. You seemed so tired when we parted."

"You're right. I was totally worn out from all the ups and downs. Rose, I think it was the most difficult day of learning I have had with you."

"Well, well," she replied, "I didn't want to lose you to discouragement in the early days. We had to save the hardest lesson for last, you see. Angela, learning to forgive yourself and others is the highest hurdle and the biggest mountain you will ever have to climb on the way to God. The Bible continually reminds us to do it, but many people continue to do it through clenched teeth, if you know what I mean." She then mimicked a feeling I'd had many times. Her teeth clenched and looking angry, she said, "I guess I'll have to forgive them, but I'm never going to forget it." Then she laughed again. "That is an example of a person who takes the action only because she knows she should. That's really a cop-out. Your heart doesn't buy it, and neither does your head. It is just words. God knows it. And deep down, you know it, too, because it plays out over and over in your thoughts." She was looking a little somber.

"Until," she turned back into Little Miss Sunshine during the pause . . . "until you become a firefighter. You go in with your pick and a fire hose. You take off the lid, uncover all those smoldering embers, and deal with them openly. You see?" she added brightly.

"You know the saying . . . It's a dirty job, but somebody has to do it! But I say . . ." with that she stood up, hopped up on the bench, and held her hand up in the air as if she were about to lead the cavalry, "it's a dirty job, and *everybody* has to do it!"

Then she hopped back down and straightened out her hat that had gone all lopsided with her latest antics. Sitting back on the bench, she then looked at me and added in a whisper, "That is . . . if they want with all their heart to know joy and be in union with God."

Then she brightened again and patted my hand excitedly. "And you learned to do it, didn't you, Angela? I'm so proud of you, you know. You have been a wonderful student."

I nodded my head slowly. Yes, last night I *had* learned to do it. *But how did she know?*

The exercise was really an eye-opener. When I looked back at the embarrassment of my childhood, I was able to see how much character it had built in me. I saw how hard my parents had worked and how that related to my strong work ethic. Rose had already shown me that I actually got what I asked for in my career, and yet I was able to go deeper into that experience and see that the new owner firing me truly released me from feeling any responsibility for his success or failure in running the company. By firing me, he had actually set me free, something I'd been begging for over the years. There were so many things that the assignment helped me reframe in my mind. And, it dawned on me that I really could face the difficulties in my life head-on. Rather than try to bury my hurts, I could actually see them in a new light. I was reflecting on my fortune in meeting Rose when her voice brought me back into our conversation.

"Always look for the blessings, my dear. Always look for the blessings!"

After that, she sat in silence for a long time. She was smiling softly and looking off in the distance. Maybe she was counting her own blessings.

Thinking back, that was exactly how she looked the first day I met her. So poised, so proper. The longer we sat there, the more she seemed like some out-of-this-world character. I could feel her transformation. Everything, the bench, the air, became noticeably warmer. A warm breeze wafted by . . . and the scent. Lavender! She was blissful and strangely illuminated in a way that made me transfixed by the beauty I could see shining out from her. I wanted to touch her, see if she was breathing, but something held me back. I was mesmerized to stillness, unable to move, yet unalarmed by it.

I had a strange feeling that she was going to disappear. Tears began to stream down my face. I looked at her with overflowing love and, at the same time, trepidation. A jumble of emotions traveled through me. I was overwhelmed with gratitude for her. The feeling was so huge; I felt it could not be contained inside my body. Then, gradually, it became less intense. The joy remained fully there inside me, and I was better able to handle the emotion. As my tears subsided, it seemed that she came slowly back to a state of humanness that allowed us to speak once again.

"Rose," I whispered, "I felt like you were going to disappear."

"I'm still here," she said sweetly, slowly.

"Rose, you wouldn't leave me?" I questioned, feeling anxious but trying not to let her see it. "You're my lifeline. I don't know if I could make it without you."

She looked over at me with great understanding and yet with complete conviction in her belief otherwise. "I am not your lifeline, Angela," she said with authority. Then she added with kindness, "You know that, dear. Your answers are all inside of you. The Holy Spirit is waiting there to be your guide. Right inside," she assured me, as she reached over with her index finger and tapped lightly on my chest. "Waiting for you to hear. *Now* you can hear. You *now* know how to follow."

"Uhh . . ." I moved to protest, but she shushed me with a quick finger to her lips. And then she flashed me a huge smile full of love and fulfillment.

"Angela," she announced, "I'm simply famished. What do you say I treat you to lunch in the park? There is a wonderful little place that I bet you don't even know about! Let's do it. Just us two girls . . . It's only a short stroll. What do you say? Shall we do it?"

"Sure," I replied, "it will be a lark!" And then we both broke out in laughter at my use of the baglady's phrase.

Rose was dabbing the happy tears from her eyes with her little hanky, still smiling ear to ear as she said, "Oh, Angela, you are such a comic. That phrase is so funny being spoken by a young woman like you." She started to snicker, and then we both broke out in fits of laughter once again.

# Chapter 28

At the baglady's lead, hand in hand, we started off into the park. The day was perfect. Our path was awash in color. Azaleas of every shade lined our path. Even the hummingbirds had arrived in full force. They must have been thinking, *So many blossoms, so little time.* They were sharing space with giant yellow-and-black-striped bumblebees. The park was absolutely teeming with life.

Turning to comment on a couple of squirrels playing in an open meadow, I was taken aback to see several butterflies hovering right around Rose. One perched on her little hat as if it were a decoration specifically intended.

Another landed on her finger that she raised within inches of her face. I think she was communicating with it! Her lips were still, and she held the sweetest smile as she and the butterfly were equally focused on each other, neither showing any sense of surprise in what looked like a very unique encounter to anyone watching.

She broke her grasp on my hand and motioned me to stand still. It was then that I caught sight of the doe gazing expectantly in the direction of the baglady. It was so sweet. As Rose came closer, another deer stepped into sight. Rose knelt down beside them and stroked the head of one, as the second one leaned in so that her head was brushing the side of the baglady's hand. Standing there watching, I was in awe of the sheer beauty of these creatures, and my eyes began to mist over. How I wish I had had a camera. It was a sight to behold—the baglady, the deer and the butterfly adorning her hat.

When she returned to where I was standing, Rose once again clasped my hand and took up walking. She was swinging our arms back and forth with the innocence of a small child. "Life is such a glorious, wonderful, stupendous lark, isn't it, Angela?"

What do you say to a person after you've witnessed such

an unusual event? She gave no explanation, and I was too dumbfounded to speak. As we continued on our stroll, I noticed that everyone we passed looked our way . . . more specifically, I think they were looking reverently at Rose. Each one smiled, and some even offered a few pleasant words as we passed. It was as if Rose knew every person, every leaf and flower, every life form. I was surely enjoying our time together, but Rose . . . she was relishing this day with a completeness that I had never seen anyone demonstrate before. She was totally in the present moment.

Soon there was a fork in the path, and Rose guided me to the left, around a little bend. A few steps later, she led me off the path. For a moment, I couldn't figure out why. It seemed like we were just heading into a forest. We walked back between two huge pine trees. As we moved past them, I looked to the ground to see a flagstone path with bright green moss framing each stone. I was so taken by the naturally artistic stone placement that it held my gaze. When I looked up, we were coming up on the most beautiful stone entry. There was a natural arch, a weaving of wild grapevine cascading over the top. The scene struck me more as something Alice would have seen taking a journey through the looking glass.

Past the entry, the stone walk split off left and right. Straight in front was a beautiful pond with irises and water lilies in bloom. As we moved closer, I could hear the gentle trickle of a waterfall. And behind that, there was the melodious sound of a classical piano. Looking over at Rose with surprise and delight in my eyes, I was speechless. Imagine an outdoor café, right in the middle of the park, and yet hidden from view.

Seeing us enter, the maître d' waved at the baglady and rushed over to greet us. He immediately took her hand and kissed it as if she were royalty. "Ah, Rose," he said, "who's this lovely, young woman you have with you today?" With that, Rose introduced us, adding a short explanation about each of us in her introduction.

He took her bag and led us off the beautiful stone and moss carpet to a quiet table at the edge of the garden. I could not believe how spectacular this open-air dining room was, with the earth beneath it and the sky as its ceiling. The menu was simple—sandwiches and salads. Prices were moderate, but the ambiance was magnificent. Rose and I chatted lightheartedly throughout our meal. We hadn't ordered dessert, but the waiter brought something out, he said, "as a treat from the kitchen." The chef specifically wanted to know what Rose thought of his latest culinary creation.

When time came to pay, she reached into her bag and pulled out a little beaded coin purse, one of those with a dainty finger-twist silver clasp at the top and a gathered bag below. Both her bills and change were stuffed into it. I thanked her over and over again for such a wonderful treat on this spectacular afternoon. "You are right, Rose," I said. "I have never seen or heard of this place. It is like a living restaurant and concert hall all in one. I'm blown away by its beauty." My overflowing joy clearly delighted her. As we got up to leave, I hugged her and thanked her again.

Rose waited to speak until we had exited through the stone archway. "So, my dear, then you do think it was a fitting graduation luncheon for an exemplary student?" she asked, smiling broadly.

"Rose," I gasped, hoping I'd misheard her. "You're kidding, right? I feel like I'm still in kindergarten."

She grabbed my hand and squeezed it, then began talking as we started walking back through the park. "My dear, dear Angela. Remember this morning when I was going through my papers?" I nodded. "Well, I was checking to make sure that I had helped you with all the concepts you needed to know to become a true and happy human being, to live a life of elegance. The only thing that is left for you to do, in order to live an enchanted life, is to practice them. What you must do now is to allow the things of which we have spoken to transform your life. It is time for you to put the things you have learned into practice."

Then she added lightheartedly, "You have already started to experience the truth of all that you are. You just don't realize how far you have come. Angela, trust me, you are way past kindergarten," she laughed.

I wasn't laughing with her. "But, Rose," I started to protest. She kept right on talking, completely disregarding the panic in my voice.

"Angela, you don't want to spend the rest of your life sitting on a park bench with a little, old lady. You have places to go, people to see. You have your whole new life ahead of you," she said, spreading her arms open wide as if presenting me with the world.

Then she turned around with a flourish and took both of my hands playfully, urging me to meet her eyes. She continued, "Don't get excited, Angela. I'm not cutting you loose quite yet."

She smiled. I relaxed a little.

I could tell she was searching for a word, and then she asked, with a look of frustration on her face, "Oh, Angela, what do you call it when someone has finished their education, and they go out on their own to get the personal experience? I'm trying to think of the word."

"Apprentice?" I replied, wondering where she was going with this whole train of thought.

"Oh, yes, that's it!" She was happy at the recovery of the word. "So, let's see . . . how many days do we have left in the time you promised me?"

I had been enjoying the baglady so much that I hadn't even thought about the passing of the days. The look on my face and the shrug of my shoulders were my first indication of the changes that had truly taken place in me. Now that I thought about it, only a few short days ago I started and finished my days with fear and frustration. Since turning my attention to the teachings of the baglady, every day had become an adventure. I didn't want to lose that magic.

Just then, she answered her own question, jarring me out of my thoughts.

"Angela," she said, shaking my hands again to get my attention, "there are only three days left. Time just flies when you're having fun, doesn't it? Okay, then, for the next three days, you get to be an apprentice," she said brightly.

With that, Rose broke her grasp with my hands and curled her arm around mine as she started us walking through the park, back to where my formal education with her had started.

# Chapter 29

The walk back was once again filled with a magical sensation. The butterflies returned. We met many people passing on the path, and each one smiled; some commented on the beautiful day. Their attention was always drawn to Rose. One old gent tipped his hat to her, a sparkle in his eye. She responded warmly.

Funny, my experiences over the years in this same park had been what I always thought as typical for big cities. People usually looked away or focused their eyes somewhere else so as not to engage. But with Rose, the whole park, all its wild inhabitants as well as the people, seemed to somehow know her. The whole area came alive simply by her walking through it.

I could wait no longer. I had to ask her. Strolling through the park, her arm still linked in mine, I asked her with a true yearning to understand, "Rose, everyone seems to know you, even the animals in the park. It is as if you have the world at your feet. I have never seen anything like it. Everything responds to your presence in a most engaging way." I hesitated and then continued tentatively in a whisper, "Are . . . are you . . . an angel?"

With that, she broke her hold on my arm and started laughing. I must have really struck her funny bone because she showed no sign of stopping. She wasn't mocking me; it was more the shock of my question that had her going. She walked a few steps to a nearby park bench and sat down to collect herself. I watched her curiously, laughing along with her, but much more subdued compared to the baglady. My query had put her in absolute stitches.

Still tickled, but finally able to talk, she said, "Oh, Angela, of all the questions in the world, I never, in a million years, would have expected that one to come out of your mouth." She laughed some more and then continued,

"No . . . no . . . I'm not an angel. I'm as ornery as they come," she added with a sparkle in her eye.

"Then, Rose, please tell me, how is it that all the people are drawn to you, in the park, in the restaurant?" I continued, laying out evidence to support my case. "The animals, the butterflies, even the timid deer are intimately familiar with you."

"Oh . . . I see now what you are asking," she exclaimed. "But, my dear . . . the answer is difficult, you see." She looked very serious as she continued, "But only because it is so simple." Then she paused to leave time so the answer could stand separate from the rest of the conversation. A childlike innocence mixed with the wisdom of the ages shone in her clear blue eyes as she met my gaze.

"I love them," she said with sincerity.

Then immediately she became rather feisty. "Before you get all hearts and flowers running around in your mind, let me put that idea to rest. It's not that kind of love that I'm talking about. It is more like a deep appreciation for their part in God's universe. Over the years, I have come to appreciate the sacredness in people, animals, and all the miraculous things that God has gifted us with on our amazing planet.

"Most people are so busy rushing here and there that they don't consciously focus their appreciation outward. For anyone who takes the time to see it, all God's creatures are deserving of our love, and so loved, they return blessings in kind.

"But I am not special, my dear. I'm no more angel than the man in the moon," she exclaimed. "The entire secret, I promise you, Angela, is recognizing . . . and being grateful for . . . the gift. This gift is free to all of us. You, me, and the chimney sweep!" she said with a smile.

With that, she got up, grabbed my hand, and off we went like two little girls again, our arms swinging as we walked. The sunny day, the trees and shrubs were all so full of life, and the baglady was determined to enjoy every minute of it.

After a while, Rose broke the silence. "Angela, do you remember the lesson where you spent your day consciously recognizing that everything is God's? Remember the joy you experienced? How happy you were? Well, if you live inside that truth day by day, soon, everything and everyone you come into contact with will start to respond to the love that you project and reflect it back to you. That is what you were seeing in the animals and the people we met today. Right now, it may seem like magic to you, but soon, as you practice what you have learned, you will find that the world responds to you in a similar way.

"All you have to do is practice these truths until they become second nature. My dear, that is what makes all the difference. The way the people and the circumstances of life respond to you is a direct reflection of the attitude with which you approach your life and everything in it."

We walked a little farther, then she added, "Oh, Angela, life is truly wonderful, isn't it?"

# Chapter 30

As we arrived back at our bench, Rose was anxious to get back to work on our lessons. "Angela," she said, as she turned attentively toward me, "you really are ready to get on with your life. Believe me when I tell you that, please. I know it's true." Rose spoke with such conviction that it gave me confidence just hearing the words.

"Look at how far you have come. When we met, you were in the pits of despair. Now you come bouncing around the corner looking forward to each day."

"But, Rose, that's because I can spend them with you."

"Yes, yes, I know that's what you are thinking. You are associating your happiness with my presence in your life. Certainly, I've helped you to see some things differently. But my dear, it is you who have changed—on the inside." Then she squeezed my hand for extra emphasis. "You are now ready to start a whole new life."

She could see that my chin was quivering. Rose moved her fragile, little hands to place them on my cheeks. Cradling my head, she consoled me with her words.

"It's natural to feel a little bit apprehensive, at first. You're going to be just fine." With that, she removed her hands and wrapped me in the warmth of a hug until I got my composure back.

As she sat back in place on the bench, Rose became animated and cheerful. "So, Angela, for the next three days, you will get an opportunity to be on your own. Since you set aside this entire week, you don't have any set plans for the next few days. So you are free to 'go with the flow' as the youngsters say. It's best not to have any expectations; just enjoy each moment, no matter what it brings. Remind yourself to stay open and follow your heart. Drink in the world with all your senses. It's going to look a lot different to you than it did the first day we met. You're going to have a wonderful time. You'll see. Then, on Friday, we will meet again, and you can tell me all about your new life. How's that?"

Rose's assurances had had a positive effect on me, and I found myself looking forward to the adventure. "Okay!" I responded cheerfully. "I can do that!"

With that, she continued, "Angela, what do you say we take a few minutes to just go over anything you have questions about before I set you loose on the unsuspecting world?"

"I've got all the cards and stories here in my journal," I offered.

"Oh, yes," she replied. "That's an excellent idea. Let's leaf through them."

While we were going through them, I realized that even in the beginning when I didn't think I was listening to the baglady, she had already been imparting her wisdom.

"Rose," I said thoughtfully, "you have been such a gentle teacher. As I look back, I can see that at first, before I was even willing to listen, you were already in the process of helping me to undo all my misconstrued thinking about life. You know, I was pretty upset at first with that master-piece story. It flew in the face of everything for which I had lived my life. And then when I wanted to run away, your stories kept driving home the point that I couldn't. Nothing would change for me if I stayed the same. I didn't like what you were telling me, and quite frankly, I didn't want to hear it.

"But, somehow . . . something kept making me come back to you. And that day you told me I had gotten exactly what I asked for . . . well, that was pretty hard to take, too. I was absolutely devastated, and I felt you were just telling me that it was my own fault . . . and . . . "

She cut me off quickly with her gentle voice. "Oh, Angela, there is no fault—just experiences for learning. You were doing the best you could. Always know that. But now, with new understanding, you can choose differently in the future," she said full of cheer. "I would never want you to put blame or guilt on yourself."

"Oh, I know what you mean," I answered. "You never blamed me. The point is I was covered up in blame and self-recrimination. Since that is where I was in the moment, my ears heard based on my own guilty feelings."

I touched Rose's hand and met her eyes, saying, "Rose, you never judged me. I know that. It was all me. You know, I never thought of it like this until just now, but even in the first days, while I thought you were so vulnerable, you were really the strong one. No matter what I did . . . well . . . you know, like you were talking about just a few minutes ago . . . you loved me. And I didn't consciously realize why I kept being drawn to you. Now I can see that it was love that drew me in." My voice was breaking at the utterance of the words. "In any love I have ever known, it came with a lot of expectations. If I didn't act just right, it would be pulled away. I've seen love turn to hate very quickly in the past. Then blame and guilt would take its place. But yours is more . . . well . . . I guess I would have to say . . . it's unshakable. Just like God's unconditional love."

She was just beaming with pride as I finished the sentence. Tears were welling up in her eyes. But I knew that what she was feeling had nothing to do with what I had said about her and everything to do with the understanding of love that I had gleaned.

"Oh, Angela, you've got it, my dear. You really do understand. God's love is unshakeable, unchanging, and everlasting." She paused, and then added with a sense of awe, "It is like the sun. Every day, without fail, the sun rises to shine on everyone and everything in the world, the weak and the strong alike. It does not discriminate; decide who deserves it and who does not. The sun's light, like God's love, is there equally for everyone without fail. Be like the sun, my dear, and you will know a life of joy beyond anything you can imagine."

We chatted on awhile. I'm sure Rose knew that I was having a hard time letting her go. She was so generous to be patient and let me decide when we would part that day.

As our conversation drew to an end, we counted the days together and both confirmed that we would meet, same time, same place, on Friday. I didn't ask her about anything past Friday. I wasn't ready to hear the answer.

She wished me joy-filled days and peaceful nights. I kissed her on the cheek, and we both headed off in opposite directions. I turned once, to watch her walking away. But when I looked, she wasn't there.

# Chapter 31

As I turned back and continued walking toward home, I was unbelievably calm. After today's revelations, I was actually looking forward to what the next three days would show me. Knowing that Rose would meet with me again had relieved my earlier fear of abandonment. If a grown woman could have a security blanket, the baglady was mine.

Because of my earlier commitment of a full week dedicated to her guidance, I was able to keep my head clear to "go with the flow" for the next several days. Being a person whose time had been planned to the hour, this experience was quite freeing. Instead of being stressed by the lack of a plan, I was, for the first time in my life, energized by the whole idea.

I spent a lot of time writing in my journal that evening, making a game of my gratitude list. I decided I would write down thirty things I was grateful for. One after another, I would put down the very next thing that came into my head, no matter how trivial it seemed. After the first five or six items, I was surprised at the simple pleasures that came to my mind: days of misty rain, the smell of fresh-cut grass, coffee brewing in the morning, and watching the sunrise. Because my success and good feelings about myself had always centered on financial wealth, I was surprised by the simplicity of most of the things on my list. Of the thirty items, only a couple were dependent on money. The simple pleasures were the things I hadn't taken the time to enjoy when I was on the "merry-go-round from hell," as the baglady so eloquently called it. I hadn't even consciously taken notice of them until she entered my life. *What a blessing she has been.*

As I walked out of my building the first morning of following my heart, I reminded myself that it all belonged to God and vowed to take that thought into my entire day.

My first day as an apprentice of the baglady's wisdom turned out just fine. Nothing particularly special happened on the outside, but I felt contentment on the inside like nothing I had ever experienced before. I paid more attention and appreciated the world around me. That was quite a miraculous change in itself.

What I did notice, specifically, was that I began to feel optimistic about my future. Logically, it didn't make any sense, considering that my circumstances had not altered in the least.

That evening, I decided to write in my journal a list of things I would like to do or experience during the rest of my life. I concentrated on getting in touch with what I really and truly wanted rather than what I thought would get me back to financial security. I'd spent my whole life thinking about that already . . . and a couple days from now I could go back there if I chose. For right now, and the next couple of days, I was committed to ignoring any financial restrictions that could thwart my ability to visualize my ideal future.

My life had been far removed from what I had previously considered frivolous dreams of people without drive for success. I wanted to see what else might be inside of me by looking at the possibilities from a different perspective. Was I just a workhorse and a money-making machine, or could I really see myself with a more fulfilling lifestyle?

The second day, I began to notice that I seemed to be lucky, in small ways. I was keeping close tabs on my thoughts, and, quite to my surprise, many of the things in my thoughts would show up in my life. For example, I decided to take a walk in an unfamiliar neighborhood. At around lunchtime I started thinking that an Asiago roast beef sandwich from Panera would really hit the spot. Within five minutes, there on the right-hand side of the road was a brand-new Panera. It was just a coincidence, but I was having a lot of little coincidences like that. Each time, I had to smile. The point is, everything just seemed easy, almost effortless and stress-free.

On the third day, as I was walking through the park, I was surprised to see the mom with the "paper doll" children I had noticed at McDonald's more than a week ago. Again, they were all dressed alike. *Better to keep track of them*, I thought. The mother was at a picnic table taking things out of a grocery bag: potato chips, pop, bread, and so on. The kids were playing on the playground equipment. One of the little ones was struggling to pull herself up onto the seat of a swing. Seeing that, I stepped off the path and lifted her up. As soon as she was securely in the seat, she looked at me and smiled. "Push?" she asked hopefully. She was so cute that I couldn't resist.

I looked over toward her mother. She laughed, "She'll wear you out if you let her. Annie, tell the nice lady 'thank you.'"

I pushed Annie on the swing until she wanted to get off. Lifting her down, she immediately took my hand and pulled me toward the picnic table. I ended up having lunch with this amazing family. After we ate, Melissa and I sat and talked for a while as the kids played in the park. She had quite an interesting philosophy on life with so many kids. She told me how much it hurt her when people made comments such as "Are they all yours?" or "Don't you know what causes that?" Melissa and her husband understood that each child they were blessed with was an absolute gift from God. They were gifts for her and her husband and for each of the siblings.

She said, "I feel like living in a large family helps you to get over yourself. That's because each one grows up dealing with a lot more give and take. The kids learn the art of compromise and negotiation very early," she laughed.

"Even our little Annie knows how to speak up for herself, as you saw a little while ago. You know, I think it is impossible for anyone to continue to be rigid and uptight, and still be happy, in a large family. Everyone learns to think a little less of themselves and have more concern for the good of the whole."

Melissa told me that the people who pitied her with all those kids to take care of would be amazed at the joy she experienced every day watching them grow and learn from each other. "As parents, we give the kids a safe environment to work out their shortcomings and quirks, knowing that no matter what happens today, we are all still there for each other tomorrow."

From what Melissa was telling me, I could see that a large, close-knit family was yet another way to learn the love, forgiveness, acceptance, and surrender that the baglady was teaching me. I'd never thought of it that way before. Looking back on my family, there were also five kids, and a lot of give and take. We definitely did not get our own way all the time. Before today, I had always thought that kids in a small family really had it made. I hadn't ever even considered the advantages I had had.

Melissa had a lot of wisdom to offer. If the baglady had

not instructed me to slow down and smell the roses, I never would have taken the time to swing Annie or have a picnic with her family. I would have been too busy with my personal agenda to give them a moment's notice. And look what I would have missed.

This woman in the park with her beautiful family reminded me of all Rose was saying about everything being God's. More than ever before, I realized what a wonderful gift I had been given as a child to have a safe, loving mother and father who were committed to raising all of us to be responsible adults. As I left, Melissa thanked me over and over for spending time with them. But I felt like I was the one who had been blessed by our meeting.

On the last evening of my time alone, something really interesting happened. Robin, a guy who had traveled setting up trade shows for my company several years earlier, called me. I had not talked to him since I left the company. He sounded excited in his phone message, so I returned the call that very evening. When I reached him, he asked me if I would like to go on a trip to New York. "Sure, I would," I replied, "but . . . " I was just about to tell him all the reasons I could not afford to go, when he broke in excitedly.

"Angela, we want to take you with us. I have a ticket for you, bought and paid for. We're staying at a friend's place. I know you love New York. This is my gift to you. *Free!*" he emphasized.

During the conversation, he reminded me that several years ago I had given him a trip as a bonus, and now that he was doing so well on his own, he wanted to do something special for me.

Well, who could turn down a free trip? I was immediately excited. And what was even more interesting was that going back to New York was one of the things that I had written in my journal only a few days ago.

After I hung up, I thought of the baglady. She was going to be so amazed when I told her about this one. This New York thing was big!

# Chapter 32

I woke with excitement on Friday morning, knowing that Rose would be pleased with my experiences as her "apprentice." I could hardly wait to report all my news, especially about New York. She was anxious to hear all the details, and I could hardly contain my enthusiasm as I gave her the itinerary.

"Rose, Robin told me that the airline was running a last-minute airfare sale, so he just bought me a ticket on the spur of the moment with the others, a group of four of us that will be flying. And he's already made arrangements for a Broadway play and several other activities. There will be time for window-shopping and people-watching. We'll have a chance to do a little sightseeing, though everyone going has already spent enough time in New York to have seen all the main tourist sights. Basically, we will just do what strikes us at the moment. Knowing how much I love to travel, he said he felt pretty confident that I would want to go, so he took a chance on the ticket. Rose, I feel like I've died and gone to heaven! As it turns out, I'll be leaving tomorrow afternoon and be gone for a week."

The timing could not have been better if I had planned it. The trip gave me something to take my mind off of the fact that my days with Rose were coming to an end. I could have stayed by her side for a long time to come, but she was determined to push her baby bird out of the nest to learn to fly on her own. The trip to New York was the perfect bridge into whatever was next in my life.

Rose was tickled pink at the report, especially when I showed her that I had written in my journal that I wanted to go there. "My goodness, Angela," she exclaimed, "your prayers are being answered so quickly.

"See, that is exactly how it works," she exclaimed. "You didn't tie God up in a box. You did something very powerful when you wrote that list. You thought about what you would like and opened yourself to the possibilities for a future that would bring you happiness. And then, without even realizing it, you let go and let God. Don't you see?"

I nodded as she continued.

"You have been grateful and trusting, allowing the future to present itself to you. Rather than pushing against the current, you are already learning to go with the flow." As she said it, the baglady had spread her arms wide in excitement. "All by yourself, without any help from me, you have begun to experience the infinite grace of God that is possible when you allow him to be in charge. Isn't it glorious?"

"Yes, Rose, it really is! And I discovered something else, too. I've started to meditate. What I mean is, each evening, as I was writing in my journal, I noticed that after I was done, I just naturally felt so grateful to God that I took a few minutes to pray, thanking him for the blessing of life he has given me. In the old days, I mostly prayed for what I wanted. I hate to say this, but in a way, I guess I thought of God as a grownup's Santa Claus.

"But, Rose, now my prayers are so different and . . . I feel so much happier. For the past several days, I've just thanked him for what I do have and asked him to lead me. It has been overwhelming. I've felt so peaceful at the end of my prayers that I've found myself just sitting in the silence. One night, I sat there for more than thirty minutes. A couple of nights, the quiet would get interrupted by worries or thoughts, but then I would just go back to the thought of gratitude, and I could find the stillness again. You know, I've read about this before, but I could never do it. My mind was always running a million miles an hour. It's like everything is different now. It's so life-changing, Rose! I just can't believe it."

With that, I turned and hugged her with enthusiasm. I could hardly contain myself because I was so excited.

"Angela," she squeaked, "you're crushing me."

I let her go, checked to make sure I hadn't hurt her, and then we both laughed.

Suddenly, she started up on a completely different sub-ject, as if the previous conversation had not even taken place. "My dear, do you remember that dream you told me about? The one where each person was a light in the circle with something to give and receive? Well, I knew right then that you would only need a little nudging to remember who you really are. You didn't realize it, but that dream was a profound illustration of life. We each have people with whom we are to be involved. No circumstance is without its meaning. Know that, and you will see purpose in every aspect of your life. The most important thing you can do is to show up 100 percent in your life every day, knowing that everyone and everything in your path is there for a reason."

Then Rose stopped, and looked off to the horizon. Her gaze was soulful, as though she was questioning what to say to me next, or even whether to tell me at all. Sitting there, she took a deep breath and let it out slowly. She turned thoughtfully and took my hands in hers. "Angela, my dear . . ." She drew another measured breath before continuing. "You and I have held a spot inside each other's circle for the last couple of weeks. When I met you here on this bench, it all seemed quite by accident at first because I was only in town to look up an old friend. But, of course, nothing is really an accident," she added playfully. Returning to her serious demeanor, Rose continued, "Then the most interesting thing happened. I met you. And now I have stayed here far longer than I ever intended. Sharing a circle with you, my dear, has been such a treasure." She paused, smiling. "But now, Angela, you are off to New York and . . . and I must return to my life as well."

I know I must have registered a look of trepidation at the thought of not seeing her when I got back, but Rose continued.

"Most people miss their true life, thinking that it is off in the future somewhere or that they lost it back in the past. Be the brightest light that you can be, my dear, in every moment of your life. Imagine wonderful possibilities, and God will surely handle the details."

She paused again and then suddenly exclaimed, "My goodness, Angela, you have to get packed and ready for your trip and on with your life. You're going to be just fine, aren't you?"

"Yes, I am. I really am," I said with enthusiasm.

Changing the subject, I said, "Will you wait right here for a little while? I have to go get something."

"Sure, I won't move a muscle."

Half an hour later, I was holding a bouquet fit for Miss America as I glided toward our bench in the park one last time. Rose looked my way in surprise as I strolled down the sidewalk waving like a beauty queen. "Why, Angela, how absolutely radiant you look today," she said as I stopped at the bench. We both laughed.

"Why, no, Miss Rose Kelley, it is you who are being honored today, not me. There is no rose in the whole wide world that is more elegant than you," I said with great flair. "The judges . . . that would be me, me, and me," I teased, "knew that you already had a crown of silver hair more beautiful than anything that could be made, and yet we wanted to commemorate your coronation in a unique way to match the inner beauty and talents you have portrayed."

Placing the bouquet in her arms, I began pointing out each flower and speaking of its meaning. "Rose, all the flowers in this bouquet symbolize the beauty of your spirit and embody the wisdom you have so freely shared. Here at the top is a long-stemmed white rose, acknowledging the purity and spiritual love you exemplify in the world. The iris is for the faith, hope, and wisdom you possess. Dahlias are for your dignity and elegance. Carnations are a symbol of fascination and devoted love. The yellow rose represents joy and gladness. Mums in various colors are for your cheerfulness and innocence; the white ones stand for truth. Baby rose buds are for your heart of unconditional love. And see these tea roses? They are very special, indeed. They exemplify my promise that wherever I go, whatever I do, for the rest of my life, I'll take you with me in my heart, remembering the things you taught me."

Then I pulled out a navy blue velvet box and presented it for her approval. Inside was a delicate dove, with an olive branch in its beak. Rose sighed in delight as I pinned it on the lapel of her jacket. "Rose, you have been my dove of hope, bringing me peace after a long and difficult storm. Thank you so much," I whispered, hugging her gently this time.

Realizing that the moment of our parting was close at hand, I turned back around, not wanting to move. Rose slipped her hand into mine, bringing back the memory of the first time her gentle spirit had touched me. Tears of gratitude mixed with tears of sadness rimmed my eyes, threatening to escape in a flood. I knew we were both meant to move forward into the rest of your lives, but I wanted so much to hold on.

Knowing what was coming, Rose smartly asked, "Didn't you say you were leaving tomorrow, Angela? You need to pack."

"Rose," I said, grinning through my tears, "you're trying to change the subject so I don't have to spoil another one of your hankies, aren't you?"

"Who, me?" She smiled and reached into her bag, hand me a pretty linen handkerchief with my name embroidered on it. "This one is for you to keep," she said sweetly.

"Rose," I spoke tentatively, "could I ask you one more question before you go? Please tell me, how is it that you seem to be able to pull anything you need out of your bag at a moment's notice?"

"My dear, the more you put your life in God's hands, being grateful for everything and everyone in it, the more you will see that whatever you need will always be right there. For you, over these few short weeks, they seem to have come from this shopping bag, but the answer to your needs could come from anywhere. It could be right around the corner or in a book that, despite your efforts otherwise, chooses to open on a page you need to read. It could be a $100 bill found in the toe of a shoe, a message on a sign along the road, or a call from an old friend like you experienced yesterday.

"It is a truly magical world we live in, my dear. Live the truth of the things we have discussed. Everything you need, the paths you are to follow, the job, the associations you are to make, they will all present themselves to you.

"You have a wonderful life ahead of you, Angela," she said, patting my hand.

"Rose . . . will I ever see you again?"

"I hope so, my dear. But for right now, will you make me a promise?"

"Anything," I replied.

"Have a wonderful, fantastic trip to New York. Live fully in each moment you are there, and every moment after that until, in some distant future, we may meet again."

I nodded. We both stood and hugged each other, and I watched her as she slowly strolled into the park, carrying her huge bouquet of flowers. She had walked about ten paces when she turned around, raised her hand, and gave me her best impression of a beauty-queen wave. Then she flashed me her grin, calling out, "It's been a wonderful, glorious, fantastic lark, hasn't it, dear?"

I nodded through my tears. Then my darling, little baglady winked, turned around with a little hop, and walked out of my life . . . and into the future.

# Epilogue

**M**y mind went back to the first day we met. Concern for her safety and protecting her bag had put me in her life. She hadn't needed *my* protection. I had needed *her*. For a moment, I could see it again—the circles and the lights on the circles, the people who were meant to be drawn together in a way where everyone wins. I came to the bench while running from myself. And, as it turns out, I ran right into the arms of God embodied in the form of a little, old lady with a great big bag.

Then I thought of Logan's Grille. Under the guise of wanting a hamburger, I had been sent to Tom. In the end, we were both blessed—me by getting to experience being used, and Tom by seeing that God was there for him, too.

And I could see circles of people who had come and gone before, and circles that I was yet to be a part of. I saw the circle the baglady and I shared as well as those she would move in apart from me in the future. I saw points of lights as they multiplied and overlapped each other to form a huge, luminous sphere. And I was part of it all, close up and personal. Suddenly, I was outside as the observer, seeing it all from the perspective of an astronaut. The sphere of lights moved farther and farther away until it transformed in my vision to become the earth, all blue and green. And as I watched with fascination, against a black background of stars, there began to emerge a subtle form in which the earth was at rest. Watching longer still, it came slowly into focus. And there it was, the earth, cradled in the open hands of God.

I knew in that moment I was safe here on this sphere of blue and green, with . . . circles to be a part of . . . lives to touch and lives to be touched by . . . miracles to witness . . . dreams to fulfill.

My life, which I thought was over, in fact had only just begun in a new circle, where I could experience the truth of who I really am.

# Acknowledgments

First of all, I have to thank my personal editor, Sandy Scherschligt. As I wrote this book in rough form, it was Sandy who polished a bit here, deleted there, and helped pull the story all together for me. Daily, she encouraged me as we bounced around the ideas of where the story was going next and worked through the seemingly hundreds of drafts before we were both extremely pleased with the results. She fueled my enthusiasm and often we laughed at how emotional we'd get reading the latest chapters. More than an editor, I consider her part of my family.

Phil Burnett, a dear friend, gave me a hand to hold. And, with a saw and hammer in tow, he took care that my hundred-year-old house didn't fall down around me as I neglected everything except writing for almost a year. I don't think this book would have ever been written if not for him.

Every little thing mattered in bringing me to this point. Mona Lisa Schultz got me off my butt. She implored me to "Write the book NOW!" At my first Mega Book Seminar, Bucky Rosenbaum showed particular interest in the story before I had ever written a word of it. He is the one who made me believe it could sell. Jillian Mannis loved my project and asked me to send her the book proposal. Although neither Bucky nor Jillian became my agent, they both did much to build my belief, and I thank them both for that gift.

On my road to finding the perfect agent, Rick Frishman and Ken Browning offered great suggestions. John Kremer's help and confirmation on the steps to move forward through the publishing jungle were a huge help in a time when I was being pulled in several directions. He solidified my resolve.

Upon meeting Jill Lublin at CEO Space, she picked up her phone on a Saturday and called her agent, Nancy Ellis, on my behalf. After making the introduction, she handed the phone directly to me, and I finally found my literary agent. Nancy's personal grace and cooperative spirit made her the perfect one for me.

Peter Vegso, HCI founder, surprised me by asking me to send him my manuscript without my even making a pitch to him. HCI had always been the publisher I thought should have *The Baglady's Guide to Elegant Living*, but I never would have imagined that it would all happen so easily. Nancy worked with Peter to fashion a contract that was great for everyone and especially wonderful for a potential continuation of the Baglady series. The HCI staff, with Allison Janse heading the project, was so helpful in every aspect of bringing this book to print in a beautiful way.

As Robert Fulghum said, he learned everything he needed to know in kindergarten; I learned everything I needed to know about navigating the literary world by attending Mark Victor Hansen's Mega Book Seminars. And I am grateful to Jack Canfield who made the recommendation that I attend.

A special thanks goes to the one hundred women from around the country who agreed to read the initial manuscript and give helpful feedback as to what worked and what didn't. Their suggestions were instrumental in perfecting the the baglady's message.

As I have thanked the people who directly impacted the outcome of this book, I know that everyone who has ever touched my life has brought me to the place I am today and helped to give me the words the baglady was created to speak. I've been fortunate to be the child of parents who have loved each other for over fifty years. Dad still brings mom romantic cards and gifts on holidays. My parents instilled in all five of their children the confidence to go out into the world and make it our oyster.

Our ministers at Brookside United Methodist Church during my early years taught a message of hope that helped me grow up with a sincere belief in God's ever-abiding love for us. My mom and Aunt Dina, both women ahead of their time, introduced us to a bigger world view and an expanded vision of God that has allowed me to see him in the light of pure love. Though I had no children of my own, I have been blessed with six amazing god-children who have given me joy beyond measure.

Toby Evans, a dear friend with whom I have confided every personal shortcoming, has also shared many successes and has laughed and cried with me through it all. Thanks to Kathy Hadley for all the same but from a business and career perspective. These two women have given me the precious gift of believing in the best of me and sticking with me while I sometimes showed them my worst. There is no greater gift than that.

I thank Thich Naht Hanh, though I've never met him. He has helped me so much to see the interconnectedness of all things. Looking at it from his perspective, I see how true it is that *absolutely* every person who has ever touched my life is, in part, responsible for the message the baglady brings in this book.

If I have failed to mention you personally, please know that you are no less appreciated because of it. You have all been lights in the circles of my life, and for that, I am eternally grateful.

Dina Dove

# About the Author

*T*he *Baglady's Guide to Elegant Living* came about as a result of life-changing circumstances in the author's own life. At the age of forty, Dina Dove had been a successful businesswoman and entrepreneur for almost twenty years. How quickly things can change. At forty-one she walked into an uncertain future; broke, newly divorced, with no job, no unemployment pay, $250,000 in debt and the IRS knocking at her door. She didn't know what was going to become of her. Far from the tragic devastation that she expected, she stepped into the world empty and found a life that was magical beyond her wildest dreams. "It was as if I was swooped up into the arms of God," she explains.

At first, she thought it was just a fluke, but as the years passed, she recognized that the sudden push out of her old life gave the gift of a brand-new way of looking at the world. That new perspective changed everything. Having found the steps to true contentment, she created the *Baglady's Guide* series to share these teachings with others.

As a life coach, inspirational speaker, and workshop leader, Dina Dove is dedicated to helping others find the blessings hidden in their lives. Through the work she does, people remember who they really are at their deepest core and discover their unique path to personal fulfillment.

Dina lives in a hundred-year-old Victorian home in southeast Kansas and travels extensively throughout the United States. To meet her or learn more about her personal coaching and group programs, visit www.BagladysGuide.com.